GREEK
TRAVELMATE

compiled by
LEXUS
with
Irene M Cavoura

RICHARD DREW PUBLISHING
Glasgow

RICHARD DREW PUBLISHING LTD.
6 CLAIRMONT GARDENS
GLASGOW G3 7LW
SCOTLAND

First Published 1982
First Reprint April 1982
Second Reprint May 1984
Third Reprint May 1985
New Edition 1986
New Edition 1988
Reprinted July 1988
Reprinted 1990

ISBN 0 86267 211 2

Printed and bound in Great Britain by
Cox & Wyman Ltd.

YOUR TRAVELMATE

gives you one single easy-to-use list of useful words and phrases to help you communicate in Greek.

Built into this list are:

– Travel Tips with facts and figures which provide valuable information

– typical replies to some of the things you might want to say.

And on page 125 you'll find a list of Greek words that you'll see on signs and notices.

There is a menu reader on pages 69–71. Numbers are on pages 126–127 and the Greek alphabet is on page 128.

Your TRAVELMATE also tells you how to pronounce Greek. Just read the pronunciations as though they were English and you will communicate – although you might not sound like a native speaker.

Some notes on Greek sounds:

th is like 'th' in 'theatre' as against 'th' in 'there'

kh is pronounced like the 'ch' in Scottish 'loch'

e should be pronounced as in 'wet'

o should be pronounced as in 'hot'

Vowels in italics show which part of a word to stress.

You'll notice that a semi-colon is the Greek question mark.

Your TRAVELMATE gives the pronunciation before the actual Greek characters. And this way of writing Greek with English characters can in fact be used for telegrams etc.

a, an *e*nas, m*ee*a, *e*na [ἕνας, μία, ἕνα]
   20 drachmas a kilo *ee*kosee thraxm*e*s to keel*o*
   [εἴκοσι δραχμές τό κιλό]
abdomen ee keel*ee*a [ἡ κοιλιά]
aboard: aboard the ship/plane p*a*no sto
   pl*ee*o/aerepl*a*no [πάνω στό πλοίο/ἀεροπλάνο]
about: is he about? *ee*ne etho? [εἶναι ἐδῶ;]
   about 15 per*ee*poo th*e*ka pende [περίπου 15]
   about 2 o'clock per*ee*poo th*ee*o*ee* ora [περίπου
   2 ἡ ὥρα]
above ap*o* p*a*no [ἀπό πάνω]
abroad sto exoter*ee*ko [στό ἐξωτερικό]
absolutely! oposth*ee*pote [ὁπωσδήποτε]
accelerator to g*a*zee [τό γκάζι]
accept th*e*khome [δέχομαι]
accident *e*na theest*ee*kheema [ἕνα δυστύχημα]
   there's been an accident *e*yeene *e*na
   theest*ee*kheema [ἔγινε ἕνα δυστύχημα]
accommodation thom*a*teeo [δωμάτιο]
   we need accommodation for three *the*lome
   thom*a*teea y*ee*a tr*ee*s [θέλομε δωμάτια γιά τρεῖς]
accurate akre*ee*v*ee*s [ἀκριβής]
ache: my back aches pon*a*ee ee pl*a*tee moo
   [πονάει ἡ πλάτη μου]
across apen*a*ndee [ἀπέναντι]
   how do we get across? pos th*a* p*a*me
   apen*a*ndee? [πῶς θά πᾶμε ἀπέναντι;]
adaptor *e*na polapl*o* [ἕνα πολλαπλό]
address ee thee-*ef-th*eensee [ἡ διεύθυνση]
   will you give me your address? *th*a moo
   thosete t*ee*n thee-*ef-th*eens*ee*e sas [θά μοῦ δώσετε
   τήν διεύθυνσή σας;]
adjust ree*th*meezo [ρυθμίζω]
admission ee *ee*sothos [ἡ εἴσοδος]

advance: can we book in advance? bor*oo*me na kleesoome *the*sees apo preen? [μπορούμε νά κλείσουμε θέσεις ἀπό πρίν;]

advert m*ee*a theea*fee*meessee [μία διαφήμιση]

afraid: I'm afraid I don't know then xero [δέν ξέρω]

I'm afraid so ne [ναί]

I'm afraid not okhee [ὄχι]

after: after you meta apo sas [μετά ἀπό σᾶς]

after 2 o'clock meta tees th*ee*o ee*o*ra [μετά τίς δύο ἡ ὥρα]

afternoon to apo-yevma [τό ἀπόγευμα]

in the afternoon to apo-yevma [τό ἀπόγευμα]

good afternoon kaleesp*e*ra [καλησπέρα]

this afternoon aft*o* to apo-yevma [αὐτό τό ἀπόγευμα]

aftershave kol*o*neea xeer*ee*smatos [κολώνια ξυρίσματος]

again xan*a* [ξανά]

against enand*ee*on [ἐναντίον]

age ee eel*ee*k*ee*a [ἡ ἡλικία]

under age an*ee*leekos [ἀνήλικος]

it takes ages k*a*nnee pol*ee* *o*ra [κάνει πολύ ὥρα]

ago: a week ago teen peresm*e*nee evthom*a*tha [τήν περασμένη ἑβδομάδα]

it wasn't long ago then p*a*ee pol*ee*s keros [δέν πάει πολύς καιρός]

how long ago was that? preen poso kero ee*t*an aft*o* [πρίν πόσο καιρό ἦταν αὐτό]

agree: I agree seemfon*o* [συμφωνῶ]

garlic doesn't agree with me to sk*o*rtho then me ofel*ee* [τό σκόρδο δέν μέ ὠφελεῖ]

air o a-*e*ras [ὁ ἀέρας]

by air aeropor*ee*kos [ἀεροπορικῶς]

with air-conditioning me kleemat*ee*smo [μέ κλιματισμό]

airport to aerothr*o*meeo [τό ἀεροδρόμειο]

alarm o seenagerm*o*s [ὁ συναγερμός]

alarm clock to xeepneet*ee*ree [τό ξυπνητήρι]

alcohol to alkool [τό ἀλκοόλ]
 is it alcoholic? *ee*ne alkooleeko? [εἶναι
 ἀλκοολικό;]
alive: is he still alive? *ee*ne ak*o*ma zondan*o*s?
 [εἶναι ἀκόμα ζωντανός;]
all ola [ὅλα]
 all these people *o*lee aft*ee* ee *a*nthropee [ὅλοι
 αὐτοί οἱ ἄνθρωποι]
 that's all aft*a ee*ne ola [αὐτά εἶναι ὅλα]
 that's all wrong *ee*ne lat*h*os [εἶναι λάθος]
 all right entax*ee* [ἐντάξη]
 thank you – not at all ef-khareest*o* – parakal*o*
 [εὐχαριστῶ – παρακαλῶ]
allergic: I'm allergic to penicillin *ee*me
 aleryeek*o*s stee peneekeel*ee*nee [εἶμαι
 ἀλεργικός στή πενικιλλίνη]
allowed: is it allowed? epeetr*e*pete?
 [ἐπιτρέπεται;]
 that's not allowed aft*o* then epeetr*e*pete
 [αὐτό δέν ἐπιτρέπεται]
 allow me epeetr*e*pste moo [ἐπιτρέψτε μου]
almost sket*h*on [σχεδόν]
alone monos [μόνος]
 did you come here alone? *ee*rt*h*ate et*h*o
 monos sas? [εἴρθατε ἐδῶ μόνος σας;]
 leave me alone *a*se me *ee*seekhee [ἄσε με
 ἥσυχη]
already *ee*thee [ἤδη]
also ep*ee*sees [ἐπίσης]
alternator metaskheematee*ee*stees
 [μετασχιματιστής]
although anke [ἄνκαι]
**altogether: what does that make
 altogether?** poso kanoon ola maz*ee*? [πόσο
 κάνουν ὅλα μαζί;]
always panda [πάντα]
a.m. pro meseemvr*ee*as [πρό μεσημβρίας π.μ.]
ambassador o presvees [ὁ πρέσβυς]
ambulance to proton voeet*h*eeon [τό πρώτων
 βοηθειῶν]

....

get an ambulance! kal*e*ste to pro*t*on
voee*th*ee*o*n! [καλέστε τό πρώτων βοηθειῶν!]
» *TRAVEL TIP: to get an ambulance dial 100 for the
police*
America Ameree*k*ee ['Αμερική]
American Amereekanos [' Αμερικανός]
among meta*x*ee [μεταξύ]
amp: 15 amp fuse me*e*a asf*a*leea th*e*ka p*e*nde
amp*e*r [μιά ἀσφάλεια δέκα πέντε ἀμπέρ]
anchor ee *a*ngeera [ή ἄγκυρα]
and ke [καί]
angry *th*eemom*e*nos [θυμωμένος]
I'm very angry about it *ee*me pol*e*e
*th*eemom*e*nos yee-af*t*o [εἶμαι πολύ θυμωμένος
γι᾽ αὐτό]
please don't get angry sas parakal*o* mee
*th*eem*o*nete [σᾶς παρακαλῶ μή θυμώνετε]
animal to zo-o [τό ζῶο]
ankle o astr*a*galos [ὁ ἀστράγαλος]
anniversary: it's our anniversary eene ee
epete*e*os mas [εἶναι ή ἐπέτειός μας]
annoy: he's annoying me me enok*h*l*e*e [μέ
ἐνοχλεῖ]
it's very annoying *ee*ne pol*e*e enok*h*leeteek*o*
[εἶναι πολύ ἐνοχλητικό]
another: can we have another room?
boro*o*me na e*k*home *e*na *a*lo thom*a*teeo?
[μπορούμε νά ἔχομε ἕνα ἄλλο δωμάτειο;]
another beer, please *a*lee m*e*ea b*e*era
parakal*o* [ἄλλη μία μπύρα παρακαλῶ]
answer: what was his answer? tee
ap*a*ndeese? [τί ἀπάντησε;]
there was no answer then eep*e*erkhe
ap*a*ndeesee [δέν ὑπῆρχε ἀπάντηση]
any: have you got any bananas/butter?
e*k*hete ban*a*nes/voot*ee*ro? [ἔχετε
μπανάνες/βούτυρο;]
I haven't got any then e*k*ho ka*th*ol*o*o [δέν ἔχω
καθόλου]
anybody kan*ee*s [κανείς]

can anybody help? bor*ee* kan*ee*s na
voe*ethee*see? [μπορεῖ κανείς νά βοηθήσει;]
anything oteeth*ee*pote [ὁτιδήποτε]
   I don't want anything then *the*lo te*e*pote [δέν
   θέλω τίποτε]
aperitif *e*na aperit*i*f [ἕνα ἀπεριτίφ]
apology: please accept my apologies zeet*o*
   seegn*o*mee [ζητῶ συγγνώμη]
   I want an apology *the*lo na moo zeet*ee*sete
   seegn*o*mee [θέλω νά μοῦ ζητήσετε συγγνώμη]
appendicitis sko-leeko-eeth*ee*tees
   [σκωληκοειδῑτις]
appetite *o*rex*ee* [ὅρεξη]
   I've lost my appetite ekhasa teen *o*rex*ee* moo
   [ἔχασα τήν ὅρεξή μου]
apple *e*na m*ee*lo [ἕνα μῆλο]
application form m*ee*a et*ee*see [μία αἴτηση]
appointment: can I make an appointment?
   boro na kl*ee*sso *e*na ranver*oo*? [μπορῶ νά
   κλείσω ἕνα ραντεβού;]
apricot *e*na ver*ee*koko [ἕνα βερύκοκκο]
April Apr*ee*leeos ['Απρίλιος]
aqualung booka*l*es oxigo*noo* [μπουκάλες
   ὀξυγόνου]
archaeology arkheo-loy*ee*a [ἀρχαιολογία]
area ee pere*e*ok*hee* [ἡ περιοχή]
   in the area steen pere*e*ok*hee* [στήν περιοχή]
arm to kher*ee* [τό χέρι]
around *see* **about**
arrange: will you arrange it? *th*a to
   kanon*ee*sete? [θά τό κανονίσετε;]
   it's all arranged ola *ee*ne kanoneezm*e*na [ὅλα
   εἶναι κανονισμένα]
arrest *(verb)* seelamva*no* [συλλαμβάνω]
   he's been arrested ton seela*v*ane [τόν
   συλλάβανε]
arrival ee *a*feex*ee* [ἡ ἄφιξη]
arrive f*th*a*no* [φθάνω]
   we only arrived yesterday f*th*a-same m*o*lees
   kh*th*es [φθάσαμε μόλις χθές]

art tekhnee [τέχνη]
art gallery moosseeo [μουσεῖο]
arthritis ar-three-teeka [ἀρθριτικά]
artificial tekhneeto [τεχνητό]
artist o kaleetekhnees [ὁ καλλιτέχνης]
as: as quickly as you can oso pio greegora
borees [ὅσο πιό γρήγορα μπορεῖς]
  as much as you can oso pio polee borees [ὅσο
  πιό πολύ μπορεῖς]
  do as I do kane otee kano ego [κάνε ὅτι κάνω
  ἐγώ]
  as you like opos thelees [ὅπως θέλεις]
ashore steeh kseera [στήν ξηρά]
ashtray ena tasakee [ἕνα τασάκι]
ask roto [ρωτῶ]
  could you ask him to ...? borees na too
  zeeteessees na ...? [μπορεῖς νά τοῦ ζητήσεις
  νά ...]
  that's not what I asked for theneene afto poo
  zeeteessa [δέν εἶναι αὐτό πού ζήτησα]
asleep: he's still asleep akomee keemate
[ἀκόμη κοιμᾶται]
asparagus sparanghee [σπαράγγι]
aspirin meea aspeereenee [μιά ἀσπιρίνη]
assistant o voeethos [ὁ βοηθός]
asthma asthma [ἄσθμα]
at: at the cafe sto zakharoplasteeo [στό
ζαχαροπλαστεῖο]
  at my hotel sto xenothokheeo moo [στό
  ξενοδοχεῖο μου]
  at one o'clock stees meea ee ora [στίς μία ἡ
  ὥρα]
Athens Atheena ['Αθήνα]
atmosphere ee atmosfera [ἡ ἀτμόσφαιρα]
attitude enas tropos [ἕνας τρόπος]
attractive oreo [ὡραῖο]
  (person) elkeesteeko [ἑλκυστικό]
  I think you're very attractive nomeezo otee
  eese polee elkeesteekee [νομίζω ὅτι εἶσαι πολύ
  ἑλκυστική]

aubergine mee*a* meleedz*a*na [μιά μελιτζάνα]
August *A*vgoostos [Αὔγουστος]
aunt ee *thee*a [ἡ θεία μου]
Australia Afstral*ee*a [Αὐστραλία]
Australian Afstral*o*s [Αὐστραλός]
authorities ee arkh*e*s [οἱ ἀρχές]
automatic *(car) e*na aft*o*mato [ἔνα αὐτόματο]
autumn: in the autumn to ft*h*eenoporo [τό
 φθινόπωρο]
away: is it far away from here? ee*n*e makree*a*
 apo tho? [εἶναι μακριά ἀπό δῶ;]
 go away! f*ee*-ye! [φύγε!]
awful tromer*o* [τρομερό]
axle o *a*xonas [ὁ ἄξωνας]
baby to mor*o* [τό μωρό]
 we'd like a baby-sitter *the*lome mee*a*
 baby-sitter [θέλομε μιά baby-σίτερ]
 » *TRAVEL TIP: baby-sitters can be hired by the hour*
  through travel agencies and hotels
back: I've got a bad back pon*a*ee ee pl*a*tee
 moo [πονάει ἡ πλάτη μου]
 I'll be back soon *th*a yee-r*ee*so greegora [θὰ
 γυρίσω γρήγορα]
 is he back? ekhee ye-r*ee*ssee? [ἔχει γυρίσει;]
 come back yee-rna pe*e*sso [γύρνα πίσω]
 can I have my money back? boro na *e*kho ta
 lef*t*a moo pe*e*sso? [μπορῶ νά ἔχω τά λεφτά μου
 πίσω;]
 I go back tomorrow *th*a pao pe*e*sso a vreeo [θά
 πάω πίσω αὔριο]
 at the back sto pe*e*sso m*e*ros [στό πίσω μέρος]
bacon bakon [μπέϊκον]
 bacon and eggs avg*a* me bakon [αὐγά μέ
 μπέϊκον]
bad *a*s-kheema [ἄσχημα]
 it's not bad then *ee*ne as-kheema [δέν εἶναι
 ἄσχημα]
 too bad pol*ee a*s-kheema [πολύ ἄσχημα]
bag ee ts*a*nda [ἡ τσάντα]
 (suitcase) ee val*ee*dsa [ἡ βαλίτσα]

....

baggage ee aposkeves [οἱ ἀποσκευές]
baker's o foornarees [ὁ φουρνάρης]
balcony to balkonee [τό μπαλκόνι]
    a room with a balcony ena thomateeo me
    balkonee [ἕνα δωμάτιο μέ μπαλκόνι]
ball ee bala [ἡ μπάλλα]
ball-point pen ena beek [ἕνα μπίκ]
banana meea banana [μιά μπανάνα]
band orkheestra [ὀρχήστρα]
bandage o epeethesmos [ὁ ἐπίδεσμος]
    could you change the bandage? boreete na
    alaxete ton epeethesmo? [μπορεῖτε νά ἀλλάξετε
    τόν ἐπίδεσμο;]
bank ee trapeza [ἡ τράπεζα]
» *TRAVEL TIP: banking hours: Mon–Fri 8.00-14.00*
   hrs; you'll need your passport at the bank; bank
   holidays see public holidays; money can also be
   changed at points of entry into Greece (24 hr
   service), at some Telecommunication Offices
   (OTE) and post offices and at some hotels and in
   tourist gift shops
   YOU MAY HEAR...
   to theeavateereeo sas parakalo *your passport*
   please
bar to bar [μπάρ]
    when does the bar open? pote aneegee to
    bar? [πότε ἀνοίγει τό μπάρ;]
barber's o korreas [ὁ κουρέας]
bargain: it's a real bargain eene
    pragmateekee efkereea [εἶναι πραγματική
    εὐκαιρία]
barmaid ee serveetora [ἡ σερβιτόρα]
barman o barman [ὁ μπάρμαν]
basket to kalathee [τό καλάθι]
bath to baneeo [τό μπάνιο]
    can I have a bath? boro na kano baneeo?
    [μπορῶ νά κάνω μπάνιο;]
    could you give me a bath towel? moo
    theenete meea petsseta baneeoo? [μου δίνετε μία
    πετσέτα μπάνιου;]

bathing to kol*ee*mbee [τό κολύμβι]
  bathing costume to ma-yo [τό μαγιό]
bathroom to lootr*o* [τό λουτρό]
  we want a room with a private bathroom
  *the*lome ena thom*a*teeo me lootr*o* [θέλομε ἕνα
  δωμάτιο μέ λουτρό]
  can I use your bathroom? boro na
  khree-ss*ee*-mo-pee-*ee*sso to lootr*o* *sas*? [μπορῶ
  νά χρησιμοποιήσω τό λουτρό σας;]
battery ee batar*ee*a [ἡ μπαταρία]
beach ee paral*ee*a [ἡ παραλία]
  see you on the beach *th*a se tho steen
  paral*ee*a [θά σέ δῶ στήν παραλία]
beans fass*o*leea [φασόλια]
beautiful or*e*os [ὡραῖος]
  that was a beautiful meal *ee*tan ena or*e*o
  ye-vma [ἦταν ἕνα ὡραῖο γεῦμα]
because epeeth*ee* [ἐπειδή]
  because of the weather lo*g*o too ker*oo* [λόγω
  τοῦ καιροῦ]
bed krev*a*tee [τό κρεβάτι]
  single bed/double bed mon*o* krev*a*tee/
  th*ee*plo krev*a*tee [μονό κρεβάτι/διπλό κρεβάτι]
  you haven't changed my bed then*a*laxate to
  krev*a*tee moo [δέν ἀλλάξατε τό κρεβάτι μου]
  bed and breakfast thom*a*teeo me pro-*ee*n*o*
  [δωμάτιο μέ πρωϊνό]
  I want to go to bed *the*lo na ksaplosso [θέλω
  νά ξαπλώσω]
bedroom to eepnothom*a*teeo [τό ὑπνοδωμάτιο]
bee me*e*a m*e*leessa [μιά μέλισσα]
beef mosk*ha*ree [μοσχάρι]
beer me*e*a b*ee*ra [μιά μπύρα]
  two beers, please the*e*o b*ee*res, parakalo [δυό
  μπύρες, παρακαλῶ]
before: before breakfast preen to proeen*o*
  [πρίν τό πρωϊνό]
  before we leave preen f*ee*gome [πρίν φύγωμε]
  I haven't been here before then *e*kho
  ksan*arth*ee etho [δέν ἔχω ξανάρθει ἐδῶ]

begin: when does it begin? pote ark*hee*zee?
[πότε ἀρχίζει;]

beginner ark*ha*reeos [ἀρχάριος]

behind p*ee*sso [πίσω]

  the car behind me to aftok*ee*neeto p*ee*sso moo
[τό αὐτοκίνητο πίσω μου]

believe: I don't believe you then se peest*e*vo
[δέν σέ πιστεύω]

  I believe you se peest*e*vo [σέ πιστεύω]

bell *(in hotel)* to koot*hoo*nee [τό κουδούνι]

belong: that belongs to me ekeeno*ee*ne theek*o*
moo [ἐκεῖνο εἶναι δικό μου]

  who does this belong to? pee-a-n*oo ee*ne af*to*?
[ποιανοῦ εἶναι αὐτό;]

below k*a*to [κάτω]

belt ee z*o*nee [ἡ ζώνη]

bend *(noun: in road)* ee strof*ee* [ἡ στροφή]

berries m*oo*ra [μούρα]

berth *(on ship)* mee*a* kl*ee*nee [μιά κλίνη]

beside thee*pla* [δίπλα]

best pol*ee* kal*ee*teros [πολύ καλλίτερος]

  it's the best holiday I've ever had *ee*ne ee
kal*ee*teres thee*a*kop*es* poo *ee*kha pot*e* [εἶναι οἱ
καλλίτερες διακοπές πού εἶχα ποτέ]

better kal*ee*tera [καλλίτερα]

  haven't you got anything better? then
ekhete t*ee*pote kal*ee*tero? [δέν ἔχετε τίποτε
καλλίτερο;]

  are you feeling better? es-*tha*neste
kal*ee*tera? [αἰσθάνεστε καλλίτερα;]

  I'm feeling a lot better es-*tha*nome pol*ee*
kal*ee*tera [αἰσθάνομαι πολύ καλλίτερα]

between metax*ee* [μεταξύ]

beyond p*e*ra [πέρα]

bicycle *e*na poth*ee*lato [ἕνα ποδήλατο]

  can we hire bicycles here? bor*oo*me na
neek*ee*a-*so*me poth*ee*lata eth*o*? [μπορούμε νά
νοικιάσωμε ποδήλατα ἐδῶ;]

big meg*a*lo [μεγάλο]

  a big one *e*na meg*a*lo [ἕνα μεγάλο]

that's too big eene polee megalo [εἶναι πολύ
μεγάλο]
it's not big enough then eene arketa megalo
[δέν εἶναι ἀρκετά μεγάλο]
have you got a bigger one? ekhete ena
megaleetero? [ἔχετε ἕνα μεγαλλίτερο;]
bikini to bikini [τό μπικίνι]
bill o logareeasmos [ὁ λογαριασμός]
   could I have the bill, please? boro na ekho
   ton logareeasmo, parakalo? [μπορῶ νά ἔχω τόν
   λογαριασμό, παρακαλῶ;]
bird to poolee [τό πουλί]
birthday ta ye-nethleea [τά γενέθλια]
   happy birthday khroneea polla [χρόνια
   πολλά]
   it's my birthday eene ta yenethleea moo [εἶναι
   τά γενέθλια μου]
biscuit beeskoto [μπισκότο]
bit: just a little bit for me mono leego ya mena
[μόνο λίγο γιά μένα]
   that's a bit too expensive afto eene kapos
   polee akreevo [αὐτό εἶναι κάπως πολύ ἀκριβό]
   a bit of that cake leego apo afto to cake [λίγο
   ἀπό αὐτό τό κέἴκ]
   a big bit ena megalo komatee [ἕνα μεγάλο
   κομμάτι]
bite: I've been bitten me thaghasse [μέ
δάγκασε]
   (by insect) me tsseembeesse [μέ στίμπησε]
bitter *(taste)* peekro [πικρό]
black mavro [μαῦρο]
   he's had a blackout leepotheemeesse
   [λιποθύμησε]
bland ee-pee-os [ἤπιος]
blanket ee kooverta [ἡ κουβέρτα]
   I'd like another blanket tha eethela alee
   meea kooberta [θά εἴθελα ἄλλη μία κουβέρτα]
bleach ee khlo-reenee [ἡ χλωρίνη]
bleed emorago [αἱμοραγῶ]
   he's bleeding emoragee [αἱμοραγεῖ]

bless you *(after sneeze)* ya soo [γειά σου]
blind teeflos [τυφλός]
 blind spot seemeeo khorees oratoteeta
  [σημείο χωρίς όρατότητα]
blister ee fooska*l*a [ή φουσκάλα]
blocked fragm*e*nos [φραγμένος]
blonde *(noun)* ksan*t*hee [ξανθή]
blood to ema [τό αἷμα]
 his blood group is . . . ee om*a*tha too *e*matos
  too*e*ene . . . [ή ὁμάδα τοῦ αἷματός του εἶναι . . .]
 I've got high blood pressure *e*kho psee*lee*
  pee-essee [ἔχω ψηλή πίεση]
 he needs a blood transfusion khree*a*zete
  meta-ngheessee *e*matos [χρειάζεται μετάγγιση
  αἷματος]
bloody mary ena bloody mary [ἔνα μπλάντη
  Μαίρη]
blouse ee blo*o*sa [ή μπλούζα]
» *TRAVEL TIP: blouse sizes*

UK:	32	34	36	38	40
Greece	42	44	46	48	50

blue ble [μπλέ]
board: full board pl*e*erees theea-tro*fee* [πλήρης
  διατροφή]
 half board eemee-theea-tro*fee* [ἠμιδιατροφή]
 boarding pass thelt*ee*o epeevee*va*sseos
  [δελτείο ἐπιβιβάσεως]
boat to pl*e*eo [τό πλοῖο]
 when is the next boat to . . .? pote *e*ene to
  epomeno pl*e*eo ya . . .? [πότε εἶναι τό ἐπόμενο
  πλοῖο γιά . . .;]
body to s*o*ma [τό σῶμα]
 (corpse) ena pt*o*ma [ἔνα πτῶμα]
boil *(noun)* ena spee*ree* [ἔνα σπυρί]
 do we have to boil the water? khree*a*zete na
  vr*a*some to nero? [χρειάζεται νά βράζωμε τό
  νερό;]
 boiled egg vrasst*o* avgo [βραστό αὐγό]
bone ena k*o*kalo [ἔνα κόκκαλο]
bonnet *(car)* to kapo [τό καπό]

book to veev*lee*o [τό βιβλίο]
   booking office to praktor*ee*o [τό πρακτορεῖο]
   can I book a seat for . . .? bo*ro* na k*lee*sso
   me*ea the*ssee ya . . .? [μπορῶ νά κλίσω μιά θέση
   γιά . . .;]
bookshop ena vee-vlee-o-po-*lee*o [ἕνα
   βιβλιοπωλεῖο]
» *TRAVEL TIP: except for in the very expensive*
   restaurants it is not customary to book tables in
   Greece
boot ee *bo*ta [ἡ μπότα]
   (car) to port bagh*a*z [τό πόρτ μπαγκάζ]
booze po*to* [ποτό]
   I had too much booze last night eepeea po*lee*
   po*to* kh-*th*es to vra*thee* [ἤπια πολύ ποτό χθές τό
   βράδυ]
border to s*ee*noro [τό σύνορο]
bored: I'm bored varee-*e*-me [βαριέμαι]
boring vare*to*s [βαρετός]
born: I was born in . . . ye-n*eeth*eeka to . . .
   [γεννήθηκα τό . . .]
   see date
borrow: can I borrow . . .? bo*ro* na
   thanees*s*to? [μπορῶ νά δανειστῶ;]
boss to afend*ee*ko [τό ἀφεντικό]
**both: ke ee th*ee*o [καί οἱ δύο]
   I'll take both of them *th*a paro ke ta th*ee*o [θά
   πάρω καί τά δύο]
bottle ena book*a*lee [ἕνα μπουκάλι]
   bottle-opener to anee-kt*ee*ree [τό ἀνοικτήρι]
bottom: at the bottom of the hill stoos
   pr*o*pothes too l*o*foo [στούς πρόποδες τοῦ λόφου]
bouncer o paleek*ara*s [ὁ παλληκαράς]
bowels ta *e*ndera [τά ἔντερα]
bowl *(noun)* ena bol [ἕνα μπόλ]
box ena koot*ee* [ἕνα κουτί]
boy to ag*o*ree [τό ἀγόρι]
boyfriend o f*ee*los [ὁ φίλος]
bra to soot*ee*-en [τό σουτιέν]
bracelet to vrakhe*o*lee [τό βραχιόλι]

brakes ta frena [τά φρένα]
    could you check the brakes? boreete na
    elen-ksete ta frena? [μπορεῖτε νά ἐλέγξετε τά
    φρένα;]`
    I had to brake suddenly eprepe na frenaro
    apotoma [ἔπρεπε νά φρενάρω ἀπότομα]
    he didn't brake then frenare [δέν φρέναρε]
brandy koneeak [κονιάκ]
bread to psomee [τό ψωμί]
    could we have some bread and butter?
    boroome na ekhome leego psomee ke leego
    vooteero? [μπορούμε νά ἔχομε λίγο ψωμί καί
    λίγο βούτυρο;]
    some more bread, please akomee leego
    psomee, parakalo [ἀκόμη λίγο ψωμί, παρακαλῶ]
break *(verb)* spazo [σπάζω]
    I think I've broken my arm nomeezo otee
    ekho spassee to kheree moo [νομίζω ὅτι ἔχω
    σπάσει τό χέρι μου]
breakable ef-thraf-sto [εὔθραυστο]
breakdown: I've had a breakdown khalase
    to aftokeeneeto moo [χάλασε τό αὐτοκίνητό μου]
    nervous breakdown nevreekos kloneesmos
    [νευρικός κλονισμός]
» *TRAVEL TIP: breakdown services; ring 104 for*
    OVELPA [ΟΒΕΛΠΑ]; *24 hour service from*
    June 15–September 30; free service given to
    foreign motorists (except parts)
breakfast to pro-ye-vma [τό πρόγευμα]
    English breakfast angleeko pro-ye-vma
    [Ἀγγλικό πρόγευμα]
breast to steethos [τό στῆθος]
breath ee anapnoee [ἡ ἀναπνοή]
    he's getting very short of breath ekhee
    thees-pneea [ἔχει δύσπνοια]
breathe anapneo [ἀναπνέω]
    I can't breathe then boro na anapnefso [δέν
    μπορῶ νά ἀναπνεύσω]
bridge ee yefeera [ἡ γέφυρα]
briefcase o khartofeelakas [ὁ χαρτοφύλακας]

**brighten up: do you think it'll brighten up
later?** nom*ee*zete *o*tee *th*a kaleeter*e*psee o
ker*o*s arg*o*tera? [νομίζετε ὅτι θά καλλιτερέψει ὁ
καιρός ἀργότερα;]
brilliant *(person)* tetrap*e*ratos [τετραπέρατος]
(idea, swimmer) lambr*o*s [λαμπρός]
bring f*e*rno [φέρνω]
   could you bring it to my hotel? bor*ee*s na to
   f*e*rees sto ksenothok*ee*o moo? [μπορεῖς νά τό
   φέρεις στό ξενοδοχεῖο μου;]
Britain Vretan*ee*a [Βρεταννία]
British Vretan*o*s [Βρεταννός]
brochure *e*na feel*a*theeo [ἕνα φυλλάδιο]
   have you got any brochures about...?
   *e*khete ka*tho*loo feel*a*theea ya ...? [ἔχετε
   καθόλου φυλλάδια γιά ...;]
broken spasm*e*no [σπασμένο]
   you've broken it to espasses [τό ἔσπασες]
   it's broken *ee*ne spasm*e*no [εἶναι σπασμένο]
   my room/car has been broken into
   parav*ee*asan to thomat*ee*o moo/aftok*ee*neeto
   moo [παραβίασαν τό δωμάτιό μου/
   αὐτοκίνητου]
brooch m*ee*a karf*ee*tssa [μιά καρφίτσα]
brother: my brother o athelf*o*s moo
   [ὁ 'αδελφός μου]
brown kaf*e*thee [καφεδί]
   brown paper khart*ee* pereetee*lee*egmatos
   [χαρτί περιτυλίγματος]
   brown hair kastan*a* mal*ee*a [καστανά μαλιά]
browse: can I just browse around? boro na
   r*ee*xo m*ee*a mat*ee*a yeero? [μπορῶ νά ρίξω μιά
   ματιά γύρω;]
bruise *(noun)* m*ee*a melan*ee*a [μιά μελανιά]
brunette *(noun)* ee melakhreen*ee*e [ἡ μελαχρινή]
brush *(noun)* m*ee*a voortsa [μιά βούρτσα]
bucket o koov*a*s [ὁ κουβᾶς]
buffet o boof*e*s [ὁ μπουφές]
building to kteer*ee*o [τό κτίριο]
bulb m*ee*a l*a*mpa [λάμπα]

....

the bulb's gone ee la mpa ka-ee-ke [ή λάμπα κάικε]

bump: he's had a bump on the head kteepeesse to kefa lee too [κτύπησε τό κεφάλι του]

bumper o pro-feelakteeras [ὁ προφυλακτήρας]

bunch of flowers ena booketo loolootheea [ἕνα μπουκέτο λουλούδια]

bunk meea kleenee [μιά κλίνη]

bunk beds koo-setes [κουσέτες]

buoy ee seemathoora [ἡ σημαδούρα]

burglar o kleftees [ὁ κλέφτης]

they've taken all my money klepsane ola moo ta lefta [κλέψανε ὅλα μου τά λεφτά]

burnt: this meat is burnt afto to kreas eene kameno [αὐτό τό κρέας εἶναι καμένο]

my arms are burnt ta khereea moo ka-ee-kane [τά χέρια μου καήκανε]

can you give me something for these burns? boreete na moo thossete ka tee yee-afta ta engha-vmata? [μπορεῖτε νά μου δώσετε κάτι γι' αὐτά τά ἐγκαύματα;]

bus to leoforeeo [τό λεωφορεῖο]

bus stop ee stassee [ἡ στάση]

could you tell me when we get there? boreete na moo peete poo tha katevo? [μπορεῖτε νά μοῦ πῆτε ποῦ θά κατέβω;]

business: I'm here on business eeme etho ya thoolee-es [εἶμαι ἐδῶ γιά δουλειές]

business trip taxeethee ya thoolee-es [ταξίδι γιά δουλειές]

none of your business! then soo peftee logos [δέν σοῦ πέφτει λόγος]

bust to steethos [τό στῆθος]

» *TRAVEL TIP: bust measurements*

UK	32	34	36	38	40
Greece	80	87	91	97	102

busy *(telephone)* apa-skho-leemeno [ἀπασχολημένο]

are you busy? eeste apa-skho-leemenos?

[εἶστε ἀπασχολημένος;]

but al*a* [ἀλλά]

  not this one but that one *o*khee aft*o* al*a*
ek*ee*no [ὄχι αὐτό ἀλλά ἐκεῖνο]

butcher's o khas*a*pees [ὁ χασάπης]

butter voot*ee*ro [βούτυρο]

button to koomb*ee* [τό κουμπί]

buy: I'll buy it *th*a to agor*a*sso [θά τό ἀγοράσω]

  where can I buy . . .? poo bor*o* n' agor*a*sso?
[ποὺ μπορῶ ν' ἀγοράσω . . .;]

by: I'm here by myself *ee*me m*o*nos moo eth*o*
[εἶμαι μόνος μου ἐδῶ]

  are you by yourself? *ee*se m*o*nos soo? [εἶσαι
μόνος σου;]

  can you do it by tomorrow? bor*ee*s na to
k*a*nees m*e*khree a*v*ree*o*? [μπορεῖς νά τό κάνεις
μέχρι αὔριο;]

  by train/car/plane me tr*e*no/aftok*ee*neet*o*/
a-eropl*a*no [μέ τραῖνο/αὐτοκίνητο/ἀεροπλάνο]

  I parked by the trees p*a*rkara kond*a* sta
th*e*nthra [πάρκαρα κοντά στά δένδρα]

  who's it made by? pe*e*os to katassk*e*vase?
[ποιός τό κατασκεύασε;]

cabaret to kabar*e* [τό καμπαρέ]

cabbage *e*na l*a*khano [ἔνα λάχανο]

cabin *(on ship)* ee kab*ee*na [ἡ καμπίνα]

cable *(noun)* to kal*o*thee*o* [τό καλώδιο]

café to zakharoplast*ee*o [τό ζαχαροπλαστεῖο]

» *TRAVEL TIP: cafés serve food and (alcoholic)
drinks; in the cities they are usually open 24
hours a day; no problem with children*

cake to 'cake' [τό κέϊκ]

  a piece of cake *e*na kom*a*tee 'cake' [ἔνα κομάτι
κέϊκ]

calculator to ko-mpee-oo-ter*a*kee [τό
κομπιουτεράκι]

call fon*a*zo [φωνάζω]

  will you call the manager? fon*a*zete ton
thee-ef-*th*eend*ee*? [φωνάζετε τόν διευθηντή;]

  what is this called? pos to l*e*ne? [πῶς τό λένε;]

call box teelefoneek*os tha*lamos [τηλεφωνικός θάλαμος]

calm *(sea)* ee*remee [ἤρεμη]

  calm down eeremeese [ἤρέμησε]

camera ee fotografeek*ee* meekhan*ee* [ἡ φωτογραφική μηχανή]

» *TRAVEL TIP: cameras in museums and archaeological sites usually permitted provided no tripod is used*

camp: is there somewhere we can camp? eep*ar*khee m*e*ros na kataskeen*o*ssome? [ὑπάρχει μέρος νά κατασκηνώσωμε;]

  can we camp here? bor*oo*me na kataskeen*o*ssome eth*o*? [μποροῦμε νά κατασκηνώσωμε ἐδῶ;]

  camping holiday katask*ee*nossee [κατασκήνωση]

  campsite 'camping' [κάμπινγκ]

» *TRAVEL TIP: there is no free camping in Greece*

can¹: a can of beer mee*a* b*ee*ra [μία μπύρα]

  can-opener to aneekt*ee*ree [τό ἀνοικτήρι]

can²: can I have . . .? boro na *e*kho . . .? [μπορῶ νά ἔχω . . .;]

  can you show me . . .? bor*ee*te na moo the*e*xete . . .? [μπορεῖτε νά μοῦ δείξετε . . .;]

  I can't . . . then boro . . . [δέν μπορῶ . . .]

  he can't . . . then bor*ee* [δέν μπορεῖ]

  we can't . . . then bor*oo*me [δέν μποροῦμε]

Canada Kanath*a*s [Καναδάς]

Canadian Kanath*o*s [Καναδός]

cancel: I want to cancel my booking *the*lo na akeeroso tee *the*ssee moo [θέλω νά ἀκυρώσω τή θέση μου]

  can we cancel dinner for tonight? bor*oo*me na akeerosome to fage*e*to ya s*ee*mera to vra*thee*? [μποροῦμε νά ἀκυρώσωμε τό φαγητό γιά σήμερα τό βράδυ;]

candle to ker*ee* [τό κερί]

capsize anapothogeer*ee*zo [ἀναποδογυρίζω]

car to aftok*ee*neeto [τό αὐτοκίνητο]

by car me aftokeeneeto [μέ αὐτοκίνητο]
carafe meea karafa [μιά καράφα]
caravan trokhospeeto [τροχόσπιτο]
carburettor to karbeerater [τό καρμπιρατέρ]
cards ee kartes [οἱ κάρτες]
  do you play cards? pezete kharteea? [παίζετε
  χαρτιά]
care: goodbye, take care adeeo ke na
  prossekhees [ἀντίο, καί νά προσέχεις]
  will you take care of this suitcase for me?
  boreete na moo prosexete aftee tee valeedza
  [μπορεῖτε νά μου πρασέξετε αὐτή τή βαλίτσα]
careful: be careful prosekhe [πρόσεχε]
car-ferry to feree [τό φέρρυ]
car park to 'parking' [τό πάρκινγκ]
carpet to khalee [τό χαλί]
carrot ena karoto [ἔνα καρόττο]
carry: will you carry this for me? boreete na
  moo seekosete afto? [μπορεῖτε νά μοῦ σηκώσετε
  αὐτό;]
  carry-cot port-bebe [πόρτ-μπεμπέ]
carving ee gleepteekee [ἡ γλυπτική]
case *(suitcase)* ee valeedza [ἡ βαλίτσα]
cash metreeta [μετρητά]
  I haven't any cash then ekho metreeta [δέν
  ἔχω μετρητά]
  cash desk to tameeo [τό ταμεῖο]
  will you cash a cheque for me? boreete na
  moo exargeerosete meea epeetagee? [μπορεῖτε
  νά μοῦ ἐξαργυρώσετε μιά ἐπιταγή;]
casino to kazeeno [τό καζίνο]
cassette kasseta [κασσέτα]
cat ee gata [ἡ γάτα]
catch: where do we catch the bus? apo poo
  tha parome to le-oforeeo? [ἀπό ποῦ θά πάρωμε τό
  λεωφορεῖο;]
  he's caught a bug koleesse meea arosteea
  [κόλλησε μιά ἀρρώστια]
cathedral o kathethreekos naos [ὁ καθεδρικός
  ναός]

catholic *(adjective)* kath*oleeka* [καθολικά]
cauliflower koonoop*ee*thee [κουνουπίδι]
cave ee speelee*a* [ἡ σπηλιά]
ceiling to tava*n*ee [τό ταβάνι]
celery s*e*leeno [σέλινο]
cellophane selof*a*n [σελοφάν]
centigrade Kels*ee*oo [Κελσίου]

» *TRAVEL TIP: to convert C to F:* $\dfrac{C}{5} \times 9 + 32 = F$

| centigrade | −5 | 0 | 10 | 15 | 21 | 30 | 36.9 |
| Fahrenheit | 23 | 32 | 50 | 59 | 70 | 86 | 98.4 |

centimetre ekatoss*t*o [ἑκατοστό]
» *TRAVEL TIP: 1 cm = 0.39 inches*
central kendreekos [κεντρικός]
  with central heating me kendree*kee*
  *ther*mansee [μέ κεντρική θέρμανση]
centre to k*e*ndro [τό κέντρο]
  how do we get to the centre? pos *th*a pame
  sto k*e*ndro tees po*l*e-os? [πῶς θά πᾶμε στό κέντρο
  τῆς πόλεως;]
certain ve*v*e-os [βέβαιος]
  are you certain? *ee*se ve*v*e-os? [εἶσαι βέβαιος;]
certificate to peesto-pee-ee-teek*o* [τό
  πιστοποιητικό]
chain ee alees*ee*etha [ἡ ἀλυσίδα]
chair ee karekla [ἡ καρέκλα]
chambermaid ee kamaree-*e*ra [ἡ καμαριέρα]
champagne samp*a*neea [σαμπάνια]
change: could you change this into
  drachmas? bor*ee*te na moo ala*x*ete aft*o* se
  thrakhm*e*s? [μπορεῖτε νά μοῦ ἀλλάξετε αὐτό σέ
  δραχμές;]
  I haven't any change then ekho psee*l*a [δέν
  ἔχω ψιλά]
  do we have to change trains? pr*e*pee na
  ala*x*ome tre*n*o? [πρέπει νά ἀλλάξωμε τραῖνο;]
  I'll just get changed *th*alaxo [θ' ἀλάξω]
» *TRAVEL TIP: changing money see* **bank**
channel: the Channel ee Mankhee [ἡ Μάγχη]
charge: what will you charge? p*o*sa *th*a

khreosete? [πόσα θά χρεώσετε;]
who's in charge? peeos eene eepef*th*eenos?
[ποιός εἶναι ὑπευθνος;]
chart o kha*rt*ees [ὁ χάρτης]
cheap f*th*eenos [φθηνός]
   have you got something cheaper? ekhete
   tee*p*ote f*th*eenotero? [ἔχετε τίποτε φθηνότερο;]
cheat: I've been cheated moo tee ska*s*ane [μοῦ
   τή σκάσανε]
check: will you check? boreete na elenxete?
   [μπορεῖτε νά ἐλέγξετε;]
   I'm sure, I've checked eeme vebe-os ekho
   elenxee [εἶμαι βέβαιος, ἔχω ἐλέγξει]
   will you check the total? boreete na elenxete
   to logareeasmo? [μπορεῖτε νά ἐλέγξετε τό
   λογαριασμό;]
cheek to ma*g*oolo [τό μάγουλο]
cheeky af*th*a*th*ees [αὐθάδης]
cheers (toast) steen eegeea soo [στήν ὑγειά σου]
   (thank you) efkhareesto [εὐχαριστῶ]
cheerio (bye-bye) ya soo [γειά σου]
   (toast) steen eegeea soo [στήν ὑγειά σου]
cheese to teeree [τό τυρί]
   say cheese khamo*g*elase [χαμογέλασε]
chef o chef [ὁ σέφ]
chemist's to farmakeeo [τό φαρμακεῖο]
cheque meea epeetegee [μιά ἐπιταγή]
   will you take a cheque? pernete eppeetages?
   [παίρνετε ἐπιταγές;]
   cheque book veevleeo epeetagon [βιβλίο
   ἐπιταγῶν]
» *TRAVEL TIP: paying by cheque is not standard*
   practice in Greece; only very big hotels, that have
   their own bank, accept cheques; see **bank**
chest to steet*h*os [τό στῆθος]
» *TRAVEL TIP: chest measurements*

UK	34	36	38	40	42	44	46
Greece	87	91	97	102	107	112	117

chewing gum masteekha [μαστίχα]
chickenpox anemovlogeea [ἀνεμοβλογιά]

child to peth*ee* [τό παιδί]
  children ta peth*ee*a [τά παιδιά]
  children's portion peth*ee*k*ee* mer*ee*tha
  [παιδική μερίδα]
» *TRAVEL TIP: only hotels giving full board or half
  board serve children's portions; restaurants
  don't*
chin to sag*o*nee [τό σαγόνι]
china porsel*a*nee [πορσελάνη]
chips pat*a*tes teegan*ee*tes [πατάτες τηγανιτές]
  (casino) m*a*rkes [μάρκες]
chocolate m*ee*a sokol*a*ta [μιά σοκολάτα]
  hot chocolate m*ee*a zest*ee* sokol*a*ta [μιά ζεστή
  σοκολάτα]
  a box of chocolates *e*na k*oo*t*ee* sokol*a*tes [ἕνα
  κουτί σοκολάτες]
choke *(car)* o a-*e*ras [ὁ ἀέρας]
chop *(noun)* m*ee*a breez*o*la [μία μπριζόλα]
  pork/lamb chop kheer*ee*n*ee*/arn*ee*ss*ee*a
  breez*o*la [χοιρινή/ἀρνίσια μπριζόλα]
Christian name *o*noma [ὄνομα]
Christmas khreest*oo*gena [Χριστούγεννα]
  happy Christmas! Kal*a* khreest*oo*gena!
  [Καλά Χριστούγεννα!]
church ee ekleess*ee*a [ἡ ἐκκλησία]
  where is the Protestant/Catholic Church?
  poo *ee*ne ee thee-amarteer*o*menee/katholeek*ee*
  ekleess*ee*a? [ποῦ εἶναι ἡ διαμαρτυρόμενη/
  καθολική ἐκκλησία;]
cider meel*ee*tees [μηλίτης]
cigar to p*oo*ro [τό ποῦρο]
cigarette to tseeg*a*ro [τό τσιγάρο]
  would you like a cigarette? *the*lete *e*na
  tseeg*a*ro? [θέλετε ἕνα τσιγάρο;]
  tipped or plain me f*ee*ltro ee me khor*ee*s
  f*ee*ltro [μέ φίλτρο ἤ μέ χωρίς φίλτρο]
cine-camera ee keen*ee*ematografee*kee*
  meekhan*ee* [ἡ κινηματογραφική μηχανή]
cinema to seenem*a* [τό σινεμά]
circle o k*ee*klos [ὁ κύκλος]

(in cinema) ee plateea [ἡ πλατεῖα]
» *TRAVEL TIP: in Greek cinemas the circle is
cheaper than the stalls*
city ee polee [ἡ πόλη]
claim *(insurance)* thee-ektheeko [διεκδικῶ]
clarify ksekathareezo [ξεκαθαρίζω]
clean *(adjective)* kathara [καθαρά]
  can I have some clean sheets? boro na ekho
  kathara sedoneea? [μπορῶ νά ἔχω καθαρά
  σεντόνια;]
  my room hasn't been cleaned today to
  thomateeo moo then kathareesteeke seemera
  [τό δωμάτιό μου δέν καθαρίστηκε σήμερα]
  it's not clean then eene katharo [δέν εἶναι
  καθαρό]
cleansing cream galaktoma kathareesmoo
  [γαλάκτωμα καθαρισμοῦ]
clear: I'm not clear about it then eeme veve-os
  yee-afto [δέν εἶμαι βέβαιος γι' αὐτό]
clever exeepnos [ἔξυπνος]
climate to kleema [τό κλίμα]
» *TRAVEL TIP: one of the best Mediterranean
climates; a short spring precedes a long, hot
summer with temperatures up to 39°C and more;
cooler on the islands; autumn, warmer than
spring, followed by a mild winter; rain in
summer unheard-of*
cloakroom gardaroba [γκαρνταρόμπα]
  (WC) ee too-aleta [ἡ τουαλέτα]
clock to roloee [τό ρολόϊ]
close¹ konda [κοντά]
  (weather) seenefeea [συννεφιά]
close²: when do you close? pote kleenete?
  [πότε κλείνετε;]
closed kleesto [κλειστό]
cloth to eefasma [τό ὕφασμα]
  (rag) ena koorelee [ἔνα κουρέλι]
clothes ta rookha [τά ροῦχα]
cloud to seenefo [τό σύννεφο]
clutch to abra-ee-az [τό ἀμπραϊάζ]

the clutch is slipping to abra-ee-*az*
pateen*a*ree [τό ἀμπραιάζ πατηνάρει]
coach to p*oo*lman [τό πούλμαν]
  coach party ee om*a*tha too p*oo*lman [ή ὀμάδα
τοῦ πούλμαν]
coast ee akt*ee* [ή ἀκτή]
  coastguard o aktof*ee*lakas [ὁ ἀκτοφύλακας]
coat to palt*o* [τό παλτό]
cockroach ee katsaree*tha* [ή κατσαρίδα]
coffee o kaf*es* [ὁ καφές]
  a coffee, please ena kaf*e* parakalo
  YOU MAY THEN HEAR...
  tee kaf*e*? *what sort of coffee?*
  eleeneek*o* kaf*e*? *Greek coffee?*
  nescaf*e*? *instant coffee?*
  me zakhar*ee* ee khor*ee*s zakhar*ee*? *with sugar
  or without sugar?*
» *TRAVEL TIP: Greek coffee is always black and
strong with a lot of grounds at the bottom of the
cup; if you'd like a white coffee ask for:*
ena kaf*e* me g*a*la
coin to kerma [τό κέρμα]
cold kree*o* [κρύο]
  I'm cold kree*o*no [κρυώνω]
  I've got a cold ekho kree*o*ssee [ἔχω κρυώσει]
collapse: he's collapsed leep*othee*meesse
[λυποθύμησε]
collar to kolar*o* [τό κολλάρο]
» *TRAVEL TIP: collar sizes*

(old) UK:	14	14½	15	15½	16	16½	17
continental:	36	37	38	39	41	42	43

collect: I want to collect... *the*lo na
maz*e*pso... [θέλω νά μαζέψω...]
  *(pick up) the*lo na paro... [θέλω νά πάρω...]
colour to khroma [τό χρώμα]
  have you any other colours? *e*khete *a*la
khromata? [ἔχετε ἄλλα χρώματα;]
comb ee kht*e*na [ή χτένα]
come *e*rkhome [ἔρχομαι]
  I come from London *e*rkhome apo to

Lontheeno [ἔρχομαι ἀπό τό Λονδῖνο]
we came here yesterday eerthame etho khthes [εἴρθαμε ἐδῶ χθές]
come on! ela tora! [ἔλα τώρα!]
come here ela etho [ἔλα ἐδῶ]
comfortable anapafteekos [ἀναπαυτικός]
it's not very comfortable then eene polee anapafteeko [δέν εἶναι πολύ ἀναπαυτικό]
Common Market ee Keenee Agora [ἡ Κοινή Αγορά]
communication cord seema kinthino [σῆμα κινδύνου]
company (business) etereea [ἑταιρία]
you're good company eese kalee parea [εἶσαι καλή παρέα]
compartment (train) to theeamereesma [τό διαμέρισμα]
compass ee peexeetha [ἡ πυξίδα]
compensation ee apozeemee-osee [ἡ ἀποζημίωση]
I demand compensation apeto apozeemee-osee [ἀπαιτῶ ἀποζημίωση]
complain paraponoome [παραπονοῦμαι]
I want to complain about my room/the waiter thelo na paraponetho ya to thomateeo moo/to serveetoro [θέλω νά παραπονεθῶ γιά τό δωμάτιό μου/τό σερβιτόρο]
have you got a complaints book? ekhete veevleeo paraponon? [ἔχετε βιβλίο παραπόνων;]
completely endelos [ἐντελῶς]
complicated: it's very complicated eene polee pereeploko [εἶναι πολύ περίπλοκο]
compliment: my compliments to the chef ta seenkhareeteereea moo sto 'chef' [τά συγχαρητήριά μου στό σέφ]
concert ee seenavleea [ἡ συναυλία]
concussion theeasseessee [διάσειση]
condition o oros [ὁ ὅρος]
it's not in very good condition then eene se

polee kalee katastasee [δέν είναι σέ πολύ καλή κατάσταση]

conference to seemvooleeo [τό συμβούλιο]

confession exomologeessee [ἐξομολόγηση]

confirm: I want to confirm ... *the*lo na epeeveve-osso ... [θέλω νά ἐπιβεβαιώσω ...]

confuse: you're confusing me me berthevees [μέ μπερδεύεις]

congratulations! seenkhareeteereea! [συγχαρητήρια!]

conjunctivitis flogosee too blefaroo [φλόγωση τοῦ βλεφάρου]

con-man apateonas [ἀπατεώνας]

connection *(travel)* seenthessee [σύνδεση]

connoisseur eetheekos [εἰδικός]

conscious: he is conscious ekhee tees estheessees too [ἔχει τίς αἰσθήσεις του]

consciousness: he's lost consciousness ekhase tees estheessees too [ἔχασε τίς αἰσθήσεις του]

constipation theeskeeleeotees [δυσκοιλιότης]

consul o proxenos [ὁ Πρόξενος]

consulate to proxeneeo [τό Προξενεῖο]

contact: how can I contact ...? pos boro na ertho se epafee me ...? [πώς μπορῶ νά ἔρθω σέ ἐπαφή μέ ...;]

contact lenses fakee epafees [φακοί ἐπαφής]

contraceptive andee-seelee-pteeko [ἀντισυληπτικό]

convenient voleeko [βολικό]

cook: the cook o mageeras [ὁ μάγειρας]

it's not cooked then eene pseemeno [δέν είναι ψημένο]

it's beautifully cooked eene orea pseemeno [είναι ὡραία ψημένο]

cooker ee koozeema [ἡ κουζίνα]

cool throsero [δροσερό]

Corfu Kerkeera [Κέρκυρα]

corkscrew to aneekhteeree [τό ἀνοικτήρι]

corn *(foot)* o kalos [ὁ κάλος]

corner ee gonee*a* [ή γωνιά]
   can we have a corner table? bor*oo*me na
   *e*khome *e*na gonee-ak*o* trapezee? [μπορούμε νά
   έχομε ένα γωνιακό τραπέζι;]
cornflakes 'cornflakes' [κορν-φλέϊκς]
correct s*o*st*o*s [σωστός]
cosmetics kaleendeek*a* [καλλυντικά]
cost: what does it cost? p*o*sa ka*nee? [πόσα
   κάνει;]
   that's too much *e*ene pol*a* [είναι πολλά]
   I'll take it *th*a to par*o* [θά τό πάρω]
cotton wool to babakee [τό μπαμπάκι]
couchette koos*se*ta [κουσέττα]
cough *(noun)* v*ee*kho [βήχω]
   cough syrup seer*o*pee ya to v*ee*kha [συρόπι
   γιά τό βήχα]
could: could you please ...? *th*a
   bor*oo*sate ...? [θά μπορούσατε ...;]
   could I have ...? bor*o* na*e*kho ...? [μπορῶ νά
   έχω ...;]
country ee kh*o*ra [ή χώρα]
   in the country steen exokh*i* [στήν έξοχή]
couple: a couple of ... *(two)* *e*na zevgaree ...
   [ἕνα ζευγάρι ...]
   (a few) mer*e*eka [μερικά]
courier seenoth*o*s [συνοδός]
course *(of meal)* pee-a*to* [πιάτο]
   of course ve*ve*os [βεβαίως]
court: I'll take you to court *th*a se pa*o* sto
   thekast*ee*reeo [θά σέ πάω στό δικαστήριο]
cousin: my cousin o ex*a*thelf*o*s moo [ὁ
   έξάδελφός μου]
cover: keep him covered sk*e*pase ton [σκεπασέ
   τον]
   cover charge engh*ee*-eess*ee* [ἐγγύηση]
cow ee agela*th*a [ή ἀγελάδα]
crab *e*na kav*oo*ree [ἕνα καβούρι]
crash: there's been a crash eg*ee*ne *e*na
   traka*re*esma [ἔγινε ἕνα τρακάρισμα]
   crash helmet to kr*a*nos [τό κράνος]

crazy trel*os* [τρελλός]
  you're crazy *ee*se trel*os* [εἶσαι τρελλός]
cream ka-eem*a*kee [καϊμάκι]
  (for skin) krema ther*ma*tos [κρέμα δέρματος]
  (colour) khr*o*ma krem [χρῶμα κρέμ]
crêche pethe*e*k*o*s sta*th*m*o*s [παιδικός σταθμός]
credit card e*th*nokarta [' Εθνοκάρτα]
Crete Kr*ee*tee [Κρήτη]
crisis kre*e*ssee [κρίση]
crisps tsseeps [τσίπς]
crossroads thee*e*asta*v*rosee [διασταύρωση]
crowded yem*a*to k*o*smo [γεμάτο κόσμο]
cruise ee kroo-a-zee-*e*ra [ή κρουαζιέρα]
crutch *(for invalid)* to thekan*ee*kee [τό δεκανίκι]
cry: don't cry mee kles [μήν κλές]
cup to fleedz*a*nee [τό φλιτζάνι]
  a cup of coffee *e*na fleedz*a*nee kafe [ἕνα
  φλιτζάνι καφέ]
cupboard to ndoolapee [τό ντουλάπι]
curry ka*ree* [κάρι]
curtains ee koort*ee*na [ή κουρτίνα]
cushion to maxeel*a*ree [τό μαξιλάρι]
Customs to telon*ee*o [τό τελωνείο]
» *TRAVEL TIP: it is illegal to take out of the country*
  stones etc you may have picked up from an
  ancient site
cut: I've cut myself kop*ee*ka [κόπηκα]
cycle: can we cycle there? bor*oo*me na
  ka*no*me poth*ee*lato ek*ee*? [μπορούμε νά κάνωμε
  ποδήλατο ἐκεῖ;]
cyclist o poth*ee*la*tees* [ὁ ποδηλάτης]
cylinder o k*ee*leen-thros [ὁ κύλινδρος]
  cylinder-head gasket fl*a*dza kapakee-*oo*
  [φλάντζα καπακιοῦ]
Cyprus K*ee*pros [Κύπρος]
dad(dy): my dad(dy) o ba*ba*s(ba*ba*kas) moo [ὁ
  μπαμπάς (μπαμπάκας) μου]
damage: I'll pay for the damage *th*a pleer*o*sso
  ya tee zeem*ee*a [θά πληρώσω γιά τή ζημιά]
  damaged katastram*e*no [καταστραμένο]

damn! na paree ee orgee! [νά πάρει ή ὀργή!]
damp ee eegraseea [ή ὑγρασία]
dance: is there a dance on? ekhee khoro? [ἔχει
χορό;]
    would you like to dance? thelete na
khorepsete? [θέλετε νά χωρέψετε;]
dangerous epeekeentheenos [ἐπικίνδυνος]
dark skoteenos [σκοτεινός]
    when does it get dark? pote skoteenee-azee?
[πότε σκοτεινιάζει;]
    dark blue ble skooro [μπλέ σκοῦρο]
darling agapee moo [ἀγάπη μου]
dashboard kadran aftokeeneetoo [καντράν
αὐτοκινήτου]
date: what's the date? posses too meenos
ekhome? [πόσες τοῦ μηνός ἔχομε;]
    can we make a date? boroome na kleessome
ena randevoo? [μποροῦμε νά κλείσωμε ἕνα
ραντεβοῦ;]
    on the fifth of May stees pende Maeeoo [στίς
πέντε Μαΐου]
    in 1951 to kheeleea eneakosseea peneenda ena
[τό χίλια ἐννεακόσια πενήντα ἕνα]
    (fruit) khoormas [χουρμάς]
daughter: my daughter ee koree moo [ή κόρη
μου]
day mera [μέρα]
dazzle: his lights were dazzling me ta fota too
me teeflonane [τά φῶτα του μέ τυφλώνανε]
dead pethamenos [παθαμένος]
deaf koofos [κουφός]
deal: it's a deal seem-fonee-same
[συμφωνήσαμε]
    will you deal with it? tha to kanoneessees?
[θά τό κανονίσεις;]
dear *(expensive)* akreevo [ἀκριβό]
    Dear Sir agapeete Keeree-e [ἀγαπητέ Κύριε]
    Dear Madam agapeetee Keeree-a [ἀγαπητή
Κυρία]
    Dear Nikos agapeete Neeko [ἀγαπητέ Νίκο]

December Thekemvreeos [Δεκέμβριος]
deck katastroma [κατάστρωμα]
   deckchair karekla katastromatos [καρέκλα
   καταστρώματος]
declare: I have nothing to declare then ekho
   teepote na theelosso [δέν ἔχω τίποτε νά δηλώσω]
deep vathees [βαθύς]
   is it deep? eene vatheea? [εἶναι βαθιά;]
defendant o kateegoroomenos [ὁ
   κατηγορούμενος]
delay: the flight was delayed ee pteessee ekhe
   katheesstereessee [ἡ πτήση εἶχε καθυστέρηση]
deliberately epeeteethes [ἐπίτηδες]
delicate *(person)* leptos [λεπτός]
delicious ye-fstee-kotatos [γευστικώτατος]
delivery: is there another mail delivery?
   tha ksanarthee o takhee-thromos? [θά ξανάρθει
   ὁ ταχυδρόμος;]
de luxe looks [λούξ]
democratic theemokrateekos [δημοκρατικός]
dent *(noun)* bathooloma [βαθούλωμα]
   you've dented my car moo trakares to
   aftokeeneeto [μοῦ τράκαρες τό αὐτοκίνητο]
dentist othondee-atros [ὀδοντίατρος]
   YOU MAY HEAR ...
   aneexte to stoma sas *open wide*
   ksevgalte to stoma sas parakalo *please rinse out*
dentures ee massela [ἡ μασέλα]
deny: I deny it to arnoome [τό ἀρνοῦμαι]
deodorant to aposmeeteeko [τό ἀποσμητικό]
departure anakhoreessee [ἀναχώρηση]
depend: it depends (on ...) exartate
   [ἐξαρτάται]
deport apelavno [ἀπελαύνω]
deposit ee prokatavolee [ἡ προκαταβολή]
   do I have to leave a deposit? prepee na
   thosso prokatavolee? [πρέπει νά δώσω
   προκαταβολή;]
depressed thleemenos [θλιμμένος]
depth to vathos [τό βάθος]

desperate: I'm desperate for a drink pethe no
ya ena poto [πεθαίνω γιά ἕνα ποτό]
dessert to epeethorpeeo [τό ἐπιδόρπιο]
destination o pro-oreesmos [ὁ προορισμός]
detergent to aporeepandeeko [τό ἀπορυπαντικό]
detour anangasteekee strofee [ἀναγκαστική
στροφή]
devalued eepoteemeemenos [ὑποτιμημένος]
develop: could you develop these? boreete na
tees emfaneessete? [μπορείτε νά τίς ἐμφανίσετε;]
diabetic theeaveeteekos [διαβητικός]
dialling code o kotheekos areethmos [ὁ κωδικός
ἀριθμός]
diamond to theeamandee [τό διαμάντι]
diarrhoea theeareea [διάρροια]
have you got something for diarrhoea?
ekhete katee ya tee theeareea? [ἔχετε κάτι γιά τή
διάρροια;]
diary to eemerologeeo [τό ἡμερολόγιο]
dictionary to lexeeko [τό λεξικό]
didn't see not
die pethe no [πεθαίνω]
he's dying pethenee [πεθαίνει]
diesel (fuel) deezel [ντίζελ]
diet thee-eta [δίαιτα]
I'm on a diet eeme se thee-eta [εἶμαι σέ δίετα]
different: they are different eene
theeaforeteekee [εἶναι διαφορετικοί]
can I have a different room? boro na ekho
ena alo thomateeo? [μπορῶ νά ἔχω ἕνα ἄλλο
δωμάτιο;]
is there a different route? eeparkhee alos
thromos? [ὑπάρχει ἄλλος δρόμος;]
difficult theeskolos [δύσκολος]
digestion khonefssee [χώνευση]
dinghy to pleeareeo [τό πλοιάριο]
dining room ee trapezareea [ἡ τραπεζαρία]
dinner to theepno [τό δεῖπνο]
(midday) to ye-vma [τό γεῦμα]
dinner jacket smokeen [σμόκιν]

direct *(adjective)* kat efthean [κάτ᾽ εὐθεῖαν]
  does it go direct? paee kat eftheean? [πάει
  κάτ᾽ εὐθεῖαν;]
dirty leromenos [λερωμένος]
disabled anapeeros [ἀνάπηρος]
disappear exafaneezome [ἐξαφανίζομαι]
  it's just disappeared molees exafaneesteeke
  [μόλις ἐξαφανίστηκε]
disappointing apogo-ee-tefteeko
  [ἀπογοητευτικό]
disco deeskotek [ντισκοτέκ]
  see you in the disco tha se tho stee deeskotek
  [θά σέ δῶ στή ντισκοτέκ]
discount ekptosee [ἔκπτωση]
disgusting seekhameno [συχαμένο]
dish *(food)* peeato [πιάτο]
dishonest then eene teemeeos [δέν εἶναι τίμιος]
disinfectant to apoleemandeeko [τό
  ἀπολυμαντικό]
dispensing chemist to farmakeeo [τό
  φαρμακεῖο]
distance ee apostasee [ἡ ἀπόσταση]
distilled water apostagmeno nero [ἀποσταγμένο
  νερό]
distress signal seema keentheenoo [σῆμα
  κινδύνου]
distributor *(car)* deestreebeeter [ντιστριμπυτέρ]
disturb: the noise is disturbing us othoreevos
  mas enokhlee [ὁ θόρυβος μᾶς ἐνοχλεῖ]
divorced khoreesmenos [χωρισμένος]
do: how do you do? khero polee [χαίρω πολύ]
  what are you doing tonight? tee kanete
  seemera to vrathee? [τί κάνετε σήμερα τό
  βράδυ;]
  how do you do it? pos to kanete? [πῶς τό
  κάνετε;]
  will you do it for me? boreete na moo to
  kanete? [μπρεῖτε νά μοῦ τό κάνετε;]
  I've never done it before then to ekho
  ksanakanee [δέν τό ἔχω ξανακάνει]

I was doing 60 kph etrekha exeenda
heeleeometra [ἔτρεχα ἑξήντα χιλιόμετρα]
doctor o ya-tros [ὁ γιατρός]
   I need a doctor khree-azome ena ya-tro
   [χρειάζομαι ἕνα γιατρό]
» TRAVEL TIP: *EEC reciprocal health agreement
   applies; get form E111 from the Post Office
   before you go*
   YOU MAY HEAR ...
   tokhete ksanapa**thee?** *have you had this before?*
   poo ponaee? *where does it hurt?*
   pernete kanena farmako? *are you taking any
   drugs?*
   parte ena/theeo apo afta *take one/two of these*
   ka**the** trees ores/ka**the** mera/theeo fores teen
   eemera *every three hours/every day/twice a day*
document to engrafo [τό ἔγγραφο]
dog o skeelos [ὁ σκύλος]
don't! mee! [μή!] *see* not
door ee porta [ἡ πόρτα]
dosage ee thossee [ἡ δόση]
double: double room ena theeplo thomateeo
   [ἕνα διπλό δωμάτιο]
   double whisky ena theeplo 'whisky' [ἕνα
   διπλό οὐΐσκι]
down: down the road para kato [πάρα κάτω]
   downstairs kato [κάτω]
   get down! kateva kato [κατέβα κάτω]
drain *(noun)* o okhetos [ὁ ὀχετός]
drawing pin meea peeneza [μιά πινέζα]
dress to foostanee [τό φουστάνι]
» TRAVEL TIP: *dress sizes*

UK	10	12	14	16	18	20
Greece	36	38	40	42	44	46

dressing gown ee roba [ἡ ρόμπα]
dressing *(for wound)* gaza [γάζα]
   (for salad) latholemono [λαδολέμονο]
drink ena poto [ἕνα ποτό]
   would you like a drink? thelete ena poto?
   [θέλετε ἕνα ποτό;]

I don't drink then p*ee*no [δέν πίνω]
is the water drinkable? to n*e*ro *ee*ne
pos*ee*mo? [τό νερό εἶναι πόσιμο;]
drive: I've been driving all day otheego*o*ssa
*o*lee m*e*ra [ὁδηγούσα ὅλη μέρα]
driver o oth*ee*g*o*s [ὁ ὁδηγός]
driving license *a*theea otheeg*ee*sseos [ἄδεια
ὁδηγήσεως]
» *TRAVEL TIP: driving in Greece: 100 kph is the
maximum speed; see also* **breakdowns,
roundabout**
drown: he's drowning pn*ee*gete [πνίγεται]
drug f*a*rmako [φάρμακο]
drunk *(adjective)* meth*ee*sm*e*nos [μεθυσμένος]
dry stegn*o*s [στεγνός]
dry-cleaner's stegnok*ath*ar*ee*sstee-reeo
[στεγνοκαθαριστήριο]
due: when is the bus due? pote *tharth*ee to
leoforeeo? [πότε θάρθει τό λεωφορεῖο;]
during kat*a* tee the*e*arkeea [κατά τή διάρκεια]
dust sk*o*nee [σκόνη]
duty-free aforolog*ee*to [ἀφορολόγητο]
dynamo to theenam*o* [τό δυναμό]
each: can we have one each? bop*oo*me na
*e*khome*e*na o k*athe*nas? [μπορούμε νά ἔχομε ἕνα
ὁ καθένας;]
how much are they each? poso *e*khee to
k*athe*na? [πόσο ἔχει τό κάθε ἕνα;]
ear to aft*ee* [τό αὐτί] **I have earache** pon*a*ee to
aft*ee* moo [πονάει τό αὐτί μου]
early nor*ee*s [νωρίς]
we want to leave a day earlier *the*lome na
f*ee*gome me*e*a m*e*ra noreetera [θέλομε νά
φύγωμε μιά μέρα νωρίτερα]
earring to skoolar*ee*kee [τό σκουλαρίκι]
east ee anatol*ee* [ἡ ἀνατολή]
Easter to P*a*s-kha [τό Πάσχα]
easy efkolos [εὔκολος]
eat trogo [τρώγω]
something to eat k*a*tee na f*a*-o [κάτι νά φάω]

egg ena avgo [ἕνα αὐγό]
Eire Noteeos Eerlanth*ee*a [Νότιος Ἰρλανδία]
either: either . . . or . . . ee . . . ee . . .
[ἤ . . . ἤ . . .]
I don't like either then mar*ee*see *oo*te to ena
*oo*te to *a*lo
[δέν μάρέσει οὔτε τό ἕνα οὔτε τό ἄλλο]
elastic elast*ee*kos [ἐλαστικός]
elastic band l*a*steekho [λάστιχο]
elbow o angh*o*nas [ὁ ἀγκώνας]
electric eelektr*ee*kos [ἠλεκτρικός]
electric fire ee eelektr*ee*k*ee* somba
[ἡ ἠλεκτρική σόμπα]
electrician o eelektr*o*logos [ὁ ἠλεκτρολόγος]
elegant komps*o*s [κομψός]
electricity eelektreesm*o*s [ἠλεκτρισμός]
else: something else k*a*tee *a*lo [κάτι ἄλλο]
somewhere else k*a*poo al*oo* [κάπου ἀλλοῦ]
who else? p-yee al*ee*? [ποιοί ἄλλοι;]
or else eeth*a*los [εἰδάλως]
embarrassed *ee*ne se ameekhan*ee*a [εἶναι σέ
ἀμηχανία]
embarrassing f*e*rnee se ameekhan*ee*a [φέρνει
σέ ἀμηχανία]
embassy ee Presv*ee*a [ἡ Πρεσβεία]
emergency ep*ee*goossa an*a*nghee [ἐπείγουσα
ἀνάγκη]
empty ath*ee*anos [ἄδειανός]
enclose: I enclose . . . essokl*ee*o [ἐσωκλείω]
end t*e*los [τέλος]
when does it end? pote tele*ee*onee? [πότε
τελειώνει;]
engaged *(telephone, toilet)* apaskhol*ee*m*e*no
[ἀπασχοληημένο]
(person) aravon*ee*asm*e*nos [ἀρραβωνιασμένος]
engagement ring ee v*e*ra [ἡ βέρρα]
engine ee meekhan*ee* [ἡ μηχανή]
engine trouble meekhan*ee*ko provl*ee*ma
[μηχανικό πρόβλημα]
England Angl*ee*a [᾿Αγγλία]

English Anglos ['Αγγλος]
enjoy: I enjoyed it very much mooaresse para
pol*ee* [μοῦ ἄρεσε πάρα πολύ]
enlargement *(photo)* megen*th*eessee
[μεγένθυση]
enormous ter*a*ssteeos [τεράστιος]
enough: thank you, that's enough
efkhar*ee*sto, fta*nee* [εὐχαριστῶ, φτάνει]
entertainment ee theeask*e*thassee
[ή διασκέδαση]
entrance ee *ee*ssothos [ή εἴσοδος]
envelope o f*a*kelos [ό φάκελλος]
equipment ergal*ee*a [ἐργαλεῖα]
error l*a*thos [λάθος]
escalator ee keel*ee*omenee sk*a*la [ή κυλιώμενη
σκάλα]
especially keer*ee*os [κυρίως]
essential vass*ee*kos [βασικός]
it is essential that . . . *ee*ne vass*ee*ko na . . .
[εἶναι βασικό νά . . .]
Europe ee Evrop*ee* [ή Εὐρώπη]
evacuate athe*e*azo [ἀδειάζω]
even: even the British akomee ke *ee* Vretan*ee*
[ἀκόμη καί οἱ Βρεταννοί]
evening to theelee*no* [τό δειλινό]
this evening seemera to apoyevma [σήμερα τό
ἀπόγευμα]
good evening kaleespera [καλησπέρα]
evening dress vrathee*no* forema [βραδυνό
φόρεμα]
ever: have you ever been to . . .? *e*khete pa*ee*
pot*e* . . .? [ἔχετε πάει ποτέ . . .;]
every ka*th*e [κάθε]
every day ka*th*e m*e*ra [κάθε μέρα]
everyone ka*th*enas [καθένας]
everything ola [ὅλα]
everywhere pand*oo* [παντοῦ]
evidence me*ea* apoth*ee*xee [μιά ἀπόδειξη]
exact akree*vee*s [ἀκριβής]
example to par*a*theegma [τό παράδειγμα]

for example paratheegmatos kharee [παραδείγματος χάρη]
excellent exokhos [ἔξοχος]
except ektos [ἐκτός]
   except me ektos apo mena [ἐκτός ἀπό μένα]
excess eepervolee [ὑπερβολή]
   excess baggage eepervaro [ὑπέρβαρο]
exchange *(money)* to seenalagma [τό συνάλλαγμα]
   (telephone) teelefoneekee seentheealexee [τηλεφωνική συνδιάλεξη]
exciting seenarpasteekos [συναρπαστικός]
excursion meea ekthromee [μιά ἐκδρομή]
excuse me *(to get past etc)* me seenkhoreete [μέ συγχωρεῖτε]
   (to get attention) sas parakalo [σᾶς παρακαλῶ]
   (apology) me seenkhoreete [μέ συγχωρεῖτε]
exhaust *(car)* ee exatmeessee [ή ἐξάτμιση]
exhausted exandleemenos [ἐξαντλημένος]
exit ee exothos [ή ἔξοδος]
expect: she's expecting eene se entheeafeeroossa [εἶναι σέ ἐνδιαφέρουσα]
expenses: it's on expenses pereelamvanlete sta exotha [περιλαμβάνεται στά ἔξοδα]
expensive akreevo [ἀκριβό]
   that's too expensive afto eene polee akreevo [αὐτό εἶναι πολύ ἀκριβό]
expert eetheekos [εἰδικός]
explain exeego [ἐξηγῶ]
   would you explain that slowly? boreete na to exeegeessete afto arga? [μπορεῖτε νά τό ἐξηγήσετε αὐτό ἀργά;]
export *(noun)* exagogee [ἐξαγωγή]
exposure meter to fotometro [τό φωτόμετρο]
extra extra [ἔξτρα]
   an extra glass/day ena poteeree extra/meea mera extra [ἕνα ποτήρι ἔξτρα/μιά μέρα ἔξτρα]
   is that extra? ekeeno eene extra? [ἐκεῖνο εἶναι ἔξτρα;]
extremely eepervoleeka [ὑπερβολικά]

eye to matee [τό μάτι]
  eyebrow to freethee [τό φρύδι]
  eyeshadow skeea matee-oo [σκιά ματιοῦ]
  eye witness o aftoptees martees [ὁ αὐτόπτης μάρτης]
face to prossopo [τό πρόσωπο]
  face mask *(diving)* ee maska [ἡ μάσκα]
fact yegonos [γεγονός]
factory to ergostasseo [τό ἐργοστάσιο]
Fahrenheit Fahrenheit [Φαρενάϊτ]

» *TRAVEL TIP: to convert F to C:* $F - 32 \times \dfrac{5}{9} = C$

Fahrenheit	32	50	59	70	86	98.4
centigrade	0	10	15	21	30	36.9

faint: she's fainted leepotheemeesse [λιποθύμησε]
fair *(fun-)* to paneegeeree [τό πανηγύρι]
  (commercial) ee ek-thessee [ἡ ἔκθεση]
  that's not fair then eene theekeo [δέν εἶναι δίκαιο]
faithfully: yours faithfully eeleekreena theekos sas [εἰλικρινά δικός σας]
fake plasto [πλαστό]
fall: he's fallen epesse [ἔπεσε]
false psefteekos [ψεύτικος]
family ee eekogeneea [ἡ οἰκογένεια]
fan *(cooling)* o anemeesteeras [ὁ ἀνεμιστήρας]
  (hand-held) ee ventaleea [ἡ βεντάλια]
  fan belt looree anemeesteera [λουρί ἀνεμιστήρα]
far makreea [μακρυά]
  is it far? eene makreea? [εἶναι μακρυά;]
  how far is it? posso makreea eene? [πόσο μακριά εἶναι;]
fare *(travel)* ta navla [τά ναῦλα]
farm to agrokteema [τό ἀγρόκτημα]
farther peeo makreea [πιό μακρυά]
fashion ee motha [ἡ μόδα]
fast greegora [γρήγορα]
  don't speak so fast mee meelas tosso greegora

[μή μιλᾶς τόσο γρήγορα]

fat *(adjective, noun)* khonthros [χοντρός]

fatally *th*anasseema [θανάσιμα]

father: my father o pateras moo [ὁ πατέρας μου]

fathom or-ya [ὀργυιά]

fault vlavee [βλάβη]

  it's not my fault then f*te*-o ego [δέν φταίω ἐγώ]

faulty elatomateeko [ἐλαττωματικό]

favourite *(adjective)* agapeemeno [ἀγαπημένο]

February Fevrooareeos [Φεβρουάριος]

fed-up: I'm fed-up *ee*me varee-esteem*e*nos [εἶμαι βαριεστημένος]

feel: I feel cold/hot/sad kreeono/zesten*o*me/ *ee*me leepeem*e*nos [κρυώνω/ζεσταίνομαι/εἶμαι λυπημένος]

  I feel like . . . *th*a *eeth*ela [θά ἤθελα]

ferry to ferry-boat [τό φέρρυμποτ]

fetch: will you come and fetch me? *tharth*ees na me parees? [θἄρθεις νά μέ πάρεις;]

fever o peeret*o*s [ὁ πυρετός]

few: only a few mono leegee [μόνο λίγοι]

  a few days l*ee*ges m*e*res [λίγες μέρες]

fiancé(e) o aravoneeasteek*o*s/ee aravoneeasteek*ee*a [ὁ ἀρραβωνιαστικός/ἡ ἀρραβωνιαστικιά]

fiddle: it's a fiddle *ee*ne apatee [εἶναι ἀπάτη]

field o khorafee [τό χωράφι]

fifty-fifty meessa-meessa [μισά-μισά]

figs s*ee*ka [σῦκα]

figure *(number)* o areeth*mos* [ἀριθμός]

  (of person) ee seeloo-eta [ἡ σιλουέττα]

  I'm watching my figure pros*e*kho t*ee* seeloo-eta moo [προσέχω τή σιλουέττα μου]

fill: fill her up gemeesse to [γέμισέ το]

  to fill in a form gem*ee*zo meea forma [γεμίζω μιά φόρμα]

fillet to feeleto [τό φιλέτο]

film to film [τό φίλμ]; **do you have this type of film?** *e*khete teteeo film? [ἔχετε τέτοιο φίλμ;]

filter *(traffic)* *f*eel*tro* [φίλτρο]
    filter or non-filter? me *f*eel*tro* ee mee khoree*s*
    *f*eel*tro*? [μέ φίλτρο ἤ μέ χωρίς φίλτρο;]
find vree*sko* [βρίσκω]
    if you find it . . . an to vree*s* [ἄν τό βρεῖς]
    I've found a . . . vree*k*a ena . . . [βρῆκα
    ἕνα . . .]
fine *(weather)* ore-o*s* [ὡραῖος]
    a 500 drachma fine penda*k*ossee-e*s*
    threkhm*es* prosteemo [500 δραχμές πρόστιμο]
    OK, that's fine enda*x*ee, seemfono [ἐντάξη,
    συμφωνῶ]
finger to tha*k*teelo [τό δάκτυλο]
    fingernail to n*ee*khee [τό νύχι]
finish: I haven't finished then tele*e*ossa [δέν
    τελείωσα]
fire: fire! foteea! [φωτιά!]
    can we light a fire here? boro*o*me na
    anapsome meea foteea etho? [μπορούμε νά
    ἀνάψωμε μιά φωτιά ἐδῶ;]
    it's not firing *(car)* then ksekeena-ee [δέν
    ξεκινάει]
    fire brigade peerosvesteek*ee* [πυροσβεστική]
    fire extinguisher o peerosvest*ee*ras
    [ὁ πυροσβεστήρας]
    » *TRAVEL TIP: dial 199 or 100*
first protos [πρῶτος]
    I was first *ee*moona protos [ἤμουνα πρῶτος]
    first aid prote*s* voeethee-e*s* [πρῶτες βοήθειες]
    first aid kit efotheea proton voeet*h*eeon
    [ἐφόδια πρῶτων βοηθειῶν]
    first name onoma [ὄνομα]
    first class *(travel etc)* protee *th*essee [πρῶτη
    θέση]
fish to psaree [τό ψάρι]
fix: can you fix it? *(arrange, repair)* boree*s* na to
    theeort*h*ossee*s*? [μπορεῖς νά τό διορθώσεις;]
fizzy me an*th*rakeeko [μέ ἀνθρακικό]
flag ee seem*e*a [ἡ σημαία]
flash *(photography)* to flash [τό φλάς]

flat *(adjective)* epeepetho [ἐπίπεδο]
   this drink is flat aft*o* to pot*o* e*e*ne
kse*th*eemasm*e*no [αὐτό τό ποτό εἶναι
ξεθυμασμένο]
   I've got a flat (tyre) m*e*peeasse l*a*ssteekho
[μ 'ἔπιασε λάστιχο]
   (apartment) to theeam*e*reesma [τό διαμέρισμα]
flavour ee ye-fssee [ἡ γεύση]
flea *e*nas ps*ee*los [ἕνας ψύλλος]
flies *(trousers)* to fermoo*a*r [τό φερμουάρ]
flight ee pt*e*essee [ἡ πτήση]
flippers ta vatrakhop*e*theela [τά
βατραχοπέδιλα]
flirt *(verb)* flert*a*ro [φλερτάρω]
float *(verb)* epeepl*e*o [ἐπιπλέω]
floor to p*a*toma [τό πάτωμα]
   on the second floor sto th*e*ftero p*a*toma [στό
δεύτερο πάτωμα]
flower to loolo*o*thee [τό λουλούδι]
flu gr*e*epee [γρίππη]
fly *(insect)* me*e*a m*e*ega [μιά μύγα]
foggy omeekhl*o*thees [ὁμιχλώδης]
follow akolo*otho* [ἀκολουθῶ]
food to fag*ee*to [τό φαγητό]
   food poisoning trofik*ee* theeleeteer*ee*assee
[τροφική δηλητηρίαση]
fool an*o*eetos [ἀνόητος]
foot to p*o*thee [τό πόδι]
» *TRAVEL TIP: 1 foot = 30.1 cm = 0.3 metres*
football *(game)* poth*o*ssfero [ποδόσφαιρο]
for ya [γιά]
forbidden apagorevm*e*no [ἀπαγορευμένο]
foreign ks*e*no [ξένο]
   foreign exchange ks*e*no seen*a*lagma [ξένο
συνάλλαγμα]
foreigner ks*e*nos [ξένος]
forget: I forget ks*e*khno [ξεχνῶ]
   I've forgotten ks*e*-kha-ssa [ξέχασα]
   don't forget mee kse-kha-ssees
[μή ξεχάσεις]

I'll never forget you then *th*a se kse-kha-sso
pote [δέν θά σέ ξεχάσω ποτέ]
fork ena peeroonee [ἕνα πηρούνι]
form *(document)* ee forma [ἡ φόρμα]
formal epeesseemo [ἐπίσημο]
fortnight th*ee*o evthoma*thes* [δυό ἑβδομάδες]
forward *(adverb)* brossta [μπροστά]
   forwarding address thee-*efth*eenssee
apostol*ee*s [διεύθυνση ἀποστολῆς]
   could you forward my mail? boreete na moo
steelete ta gramata moo? [μπορεῖτε νά μοῦ
στίλετε τά γράμματά μου;]
fracture ka*tagma* [κάταγμα]
fragile *ef-th*rafsto [εὔθραυστο]
fraud apatee [ἀπάτη]
free el*efth*eros [ἐλεύθερος]
   admission free el*efth*era *ee*ssothos [ἐλευθέρα
εἴσοδος]
freight forteeo [φορτίο]
freshen up: I want to freshen up *th*elo na
freskareesto [θέλω νά φρεσκαριστῶ]
Friday Paraskev*ee* [Παρασκευή]
fridge to pseeg*ee*o [τό ψυγεῖο]
friend o f*ee*los [ὁ φίλος]
friendly feeleeka [φιλικά]
from apo [ἀπό]
   where is it from? apo poo *ee*ne? [ἀπό ποῦ
εἶναι;]
front *(noun)* brossta [μπροστά]
   in front of you brossta soo [μπροστά σου]
   in the front brossta [μπροστά]
frost pagoneea [παγωνιά]
frozen pagomenos [παγωμένος]
fruit frooto [φροῦτο]
fry teegan*ee*zo [τηγανίζω]
   nothing fried t*ee*pote teeganeeto [τίποτε
τηγανιτό]
   fried egg avgo teeganeeto [αὐγό τηγανιτό]
   frying pan to teeganee [τό τηγάνι]
fuel ta kafsseema [τά καύσιμα]

full gem*a*tos [γεμάτος]
fun: it's fun *ee*ne theeaskethasteek*o* [εἶναι διασκεδαστικό]
funny *(strange)* peree-ergo [περίεργο]
  (comical) assteeo [ἀστεῖο]
furniture ta *e*peepla [τά ἔπιπλα]
further parapera [παραπέρα]
fuse ee asf*a*leea [ἡ ἀσφάλεια]
fuss fassar*ee*a [φασαρία]
future to m*e*lon [τό μέλλον]
  in future sto m*e*lon [στό μέλλον]
gale *thee*-ela [θύελλα]
gallon *e*na galon*ee* [ἔνα γαλόνι]
» *TRAVEL TIP: 1 gallon = 4.55 litres*
gallstone petra tees khol*ee*s [πέτρα τῆς χολῆς]
gamble khartop*e*zo [χαρτοπαίζω]
gammon zamb*o*n [ζαμπόν]
garage *(repair)* to seenerg*ee*o [τό συνεργεῖο]
  (petrol) ee venz*ee*nee [ἡ βενζίνη]
  (parking) to garaz [τό γκαράζ]
garden o k*ee*pos [ὁ κῆπος]
garlic skortho [σκόρδο]
gas to fota-er*ee*o [τό φωταέριο]
  (petrol) to gaz*ee* [τό γκάζι]
  gas cylinder m*ee*a fee-*a*lee a-er*ee*oo [μιά φιάλη ἀερίου]
gasket ee flandza [ἡ φλάντζα]
gay *(homosexual)* tee-*oo*tos [τοιοῦτος]
gear *(car)* ee takh*ee*teeta [ἡ ταχύτητα]
  (equipment) ergal*ee*a [ἐργαλεῖα]
  gearbox trouble khalasm*e*no sasm*a*n [χαλασμένο σασμάν]
  gear lever levg*e*s takheet*ee*ton [λεβγές ταχυτήτων]
  I can't get it into gear then bor*o* na v*a*lo takh*ee*teeta [δέν μπορῶ νά βάλω ταχύτητα]
gents anthr*o*n [ἀνδρῶν]
gesture kheeronom*ee*a [χειρονομία]
» *TRAVEL TIP: an outstretched open palm is a rude gesture in Greece*

get: will you get me a . . .? moo ferneteena . . .?
[μοῦ φέρνετε ἕνα . . .;]
 how do I get to the ferry? pos boro na pao sto
ferry? [πῶς μπορῶ νά πάω στό φέρυ;]
 when can I get it back? pote bopo na to paro
peesso? [πότε μπορῶ νά τό πάρω πίσω;]
 when do we get back? pote yeereezome?
[πότε γυρίζωμε;]
 where do I get off? poo katevenome? [ποῦ
κατεβαίνομε;]
 where do I get a bus for . . .? apo poo
pernome to leoforeeo ya . . .? [ἀπό ποῦ πέρνομε
τό λεωφορεῖο γιά . . .;]
 have you got . . .? ekhete . . .? [ἔχετε . . .;]
gin gin [τζίν]
 gin and tonic gin me tonic [τζίν μέ τόνικ]
ginger ale ginger ale [τζιντζερέϊλ]
girl ena koreetssee [ἕνα κορίτσι]
 my girlfriend ee feelenatha moo [ἡ φιλενάδα
μου]
give theeno [δίνω]
 will you give me . . .? moo theenete? [μοῦ
δίνετε;]
 I gave it to him too tothossa [τοῦ τὸδωσα]
glad efkhareesteemenos [εὐχαριστημένος]
glandular fever atheneekos peeretos [ἀδενικός
πυρετός]
glass to ya-lee [τό γυαλί]
 (drinking) ena poteeree [ἕνα ποτήτι]
 a glass of water ena poteeree nero [ἕνα ποτήρι
νερό]
glasses ta ya-leea [τά γυαλιά]
glue ee kola [ἡ κόλλα]
go: can I have a go? boro na prosspatheesso?
[μπορῶ νά προσπαθήσω;]
 my car won't go to aftokeeneeto moo then
ksekeenaee [τό αὐτοκίνητό μου δέν ξεκινάει]
 when does the bus go? pote tha feegee to
leoforeeo? [πότε θά φύγει τό λεωφορεῖο;]
 it/he's gone efeege [ἔφυγε]

I want to go to Delphi *the*lo na p*a*o stoos
Thelf*oo*s [θέλω νά πάω στούς Δελφούς]
I want to go *the*lo na f*ee*go [θέλω νά φύγω]
goal goal [γκόλ]
goat ee kats*ee*ka [ή κατσίκα]
  goat's cheese teer*ee* ap*o* kats*ee*ka [τυρί άπό
  κατσίκα]
God o The*o*s [ὁ Θεός]
goddess ee *the*a [ή Θεά]
gold o khree*s*s*o*s [ὁ χρυσός]
golf to golf [τό γκόλφ]
good kal*a* [καλά]
  good! kal*a*! [καλά!]
goodbye ya soo [γειά σου]
gooseberries frangoss*ta*feela
  [φραγκοστάφυλλα]
gramme to gram*a*reeo [τό γραμμάριο]
» *TRAVEL TIP: 100 grammes = approx 3½ oz*
grand *e*xokhos [ἔξοχος]
  granddaughter ee engon*ee* [ή ἐγγονή]
  grandfather o pap*oo*s [ὁ παππούς]
  grandmother ee ya-ya [ή γιαγιά]
  grandson o engon*o*s [ὁ ἐγγονός]
grapes sta*fee*leea [σταφύλια]
  grapefruit gr*a*pefruit [γκρέιπφρουτ]
  grapefruit juice kheem*o*s ap*o* gr*a*pefruit
  [χυμός άπό γκρέϊπφρουτ]
grass to khort*a*ree [τό χορτάρι]
grateful evgn*o*mon [εὐγνώμων]
  I'm very grateful to you sas*ee*me evgn*o*mon
  [σᾶς εἶμαι εὐγνώμων]
gratitude evgnomoss*ee*enee [εὐγνωμοσύνη]
gravy ee sa*l*tssa [ή σάλτσα]
grease to gra*s*so [τό γράσο]
greasy leepar*o*s [λιπαρός]
great megal*o*s [μεγάλος]
  great! *tha*vm*a*sseea! [θαυμάσια!]
Greece El*a*s [Ἑλλάς]
  in Ancient Greece steen Arkh*e*a El*a*tha [στήν
  Ἀρχαῖα Ἑλλάδα]

Greek Eleenas [Ἕλληνας]
   I don't speak Greek then meelo Eleeneeka
[δέν μιλῶ Ἑλληνικά]
   the Greeks ee Eleenes [οἱ Ἕλληνες]
greedy akhortagos [ἀχόρταγος]
green prasseeno [πράσινο]
   greengrocer's o manavees [ὁ μανάβης]
grey greezos [γκρίζος]
grocer's o bakalees [ὁ μπακάλης]
ground to ethafos [τό ἔδαφος]
   on the ground sto ethafos [στό ἔδαφος]
   on the ground floor sto eessogeeo [στό
ἰσόγειο]
group ee omatha [ἡ ὁμάδα]
   our group leader o arkheegos tees omathas
mas [ὁ ἀρχηγός τῆς ὁμάδας μας]
   I'm with the English group eeme me teen
Angleekee omatha [εἶμαι μέ τήν 'Αγγλική
ὁμάδα]
guarantee engee-eessee [ἐγγύηση]
   is there a guarantee? eeparkhee
engee-eessee? [ὑπάρχει ἐγγύηση;]
guest o feelexenoomenos [ὁ φιλοξενούμενος]
guesthouse ee pansseeon [ἡ πανσιόν]
guide o ksenagos [ὁ ξεναγός]
guilty o enokhos [ὁ ἔνοχος]
guitar ee keethara [ἡ κιθάρα]
gum *(in mouth)* to oolo [τό οὖλο]
gun to oplo [τό ὅπλο]
gynaecologist o geenekologos [ὁ γυναικολόγος]
hair ta maleea [τά μαλλιά]
   hairbrush ee voortssa [ἡ βούρτσα]
   where can I get a haircut? poo boro na kopso
ta maleea moo? [ποῦ μπορῶ νά κόψω τά μαλιά
μου;]
   is there a hairdresser's here? eeparkhee
komoteereeo etho? [ὑπάρχει κομμωτήριο ἐδῶ;]
   hair grip peeastrakee maleeon [πιαστράκι
μαλλιῶν]
half meessos [μισός]

a half portion meess*ee* mer*ee*tha [μισή μερίδα]
half an hour meess*ee* ora [μισή ώρα]
ham kheer*ee*no [χοιρινό]
  hamburger h*a*mburger [χάμπουργκερ]
hammer *e*na sfeer*ee* [ἕνα σφυρί]
hand to kh*e*ree [τό χέρι]
  handbag ee ts*a*nda [ή τσάντα]
  handbrake kheer*o*freno [τό χειρόφρενο]
handkerchief to mand*ee*lee [τό μαντήλι]
handle to kher*oo*lee [τό χερούλι]
hand luggage to sak-vooa-yaz [τό
  σάκ-βουαγιάζ]
handmade kheer*o*p*ee*-eeto [χειροποίητο]
handsome or*e*os [ὡραῖος]
hanger mee*a* krem*a*stra [μιά κρεμάστρα]
hangover: I've got a terrible hangover
  esth*a*nome ap*e*sseea met*a* to khth*e*sseeno
  meth*ee*ssee [αἰσθάνομαι ἀπαίσια μετά τό
  χθεσινό μεθύσι]
  my head is killing me to kef*a*lee moo me
  pethenee [τό κεφάλι μου μέ πεθαίνει]
happen: I don't know how it happened the
  ksero pos seen*e*vee [δέν ξέρω πῶς συνέβει]
  what's happening/happened? tee
  seemv*e*nee/seen*e*vee? [τί συμβαίνει/συνέβει;]
happy efteekheesm*e*nos [εὐτυχισμένος]
harbour to leem*a*nee [τό λιμάνι]
hard skleeros [σκληρός]
  (difficult) th*e*eskolo [δύσκολο]
  hard-boiled egg sfeekto avgo [σφικτό αὐγό]
  push hard spr*o*xe theen*a*ta [σπρῶξε δυνατά]
harm *(noun)* to kako [τό κακό]
hat to kap*e*lo [τό καπέλο]
hate: I hate ... meesso ... [μισῶ ...]
have *e*kho [ἔχω]
  I have a pain *e*kho *e*na pono [ἔχω ἕνα πόνο]
  I have no ... then *e*kho ... [δέν ἔχω ...]
  do you have any cigars/a map? *e*khete
  poora/*e*na khart*ee*? [ἔχετε πούρα/ἕνα χάρτη;]
  can I have some water/some more? boro na

....

ekho leego nero/akomee leego? [μπορῶ νά ἔχω
λίγο νερό/ἀκόμη λίγο;]
I have to leave tomorrow prepee na feego
avreeo [πρέπει νά φύγω αὔριο]
hayfever alergeekos peeretos [ἀλλεργικός
πυρετός]
he aftos [αὐτός]
  he is ... eene ... [εἶναι ...]
  he is staying at Hotel ... menee sto
  ksenothokheeo ... [μένει στό ξενοδοχεῖο ...]
head to kefalee [τό κεφάλι]
  headache ponokefalos [πονοκέφαλος]
  headlight faros [φάρος]
  head waiter arkheeserveetoros
  [ἀρχησερβιτόρος]
  head wind enanteeos anemos
  [ἐνάντιος ἄνεμος]
health eegeea [ὑγεία]
  your health! steen ee-ya soo [στήν ὑγειά σου]
healthy ee-yee-ees [ὑγιής]
hear: I can't hear then boro nakoosso [δέν
μπορῶ ν' ἀκούσω]
  hearing aid akoosteeka [ἀκουστικά]
heart ee kartheea [ἡ καρδιά]
  heart attack kartheeakee prosvolee
  [καρδιακή προσβολή]
heat zestasseea [ζεστασιά]
  heat stroke eeleeassee [ἡλίαση]
heating ee thermanssee [ἡ θέρμανση]
heavy varees [βαρύς]
heel to takoonee [τό τακούνι]
  could you put new heels on these? boreete
  na moo valete kenoorgeea takooneea safta?
  [μπορεῖτε νά βάλετε καινούργια τακούνια σ'
  αὐτά;]
height to eepsos [τό ὕψος]
hello ya soo [γεία σου]
help (noun) voeetheea [βοήθεια]
  can you help me? boreete na me
  voeetheessete? [μπορεῖτε νά μέ βοηθείσετε;]

help! v*oeeth*eea! [βoήθεια!]
her aft*ee* [αἰτή]
   I like her moo ar*e*ssee [μoῦ ἀρέσει]
   with her mazee tees [μαζύ της]
   it's her bag, it's hers *ee*ne ee tss*a*nda tees,
   *ee*ne theekee*a* tees [εἶναι ἡ τσάντα της, εἶναι
   δικιά της]
   that's hers *ee*ne theek*o* tees [εἶναι δικό της]
here etho [ἐδῶ]
   come here *e*la etho [ἔλα ἐδῶ]
high pseel*a* [ψηλά]
hill o lofos [ὁ λόφος]
   up/down the hill o an*ee*foros/o kat*ee*foros
   [ὁ ἀνήφορος/ὁ κατήφορος]
him aft*o*n [αὐτόν]
   I don't know him then ton ks*e*ro [δέν τόν
   ξέρω]
   with him mazee too [μαζύ του]
hire *see* **rent**
his: it's his drink, it's his *ee*ne to pot*o* too, *ee*ne
   theek*o* too [εἶναι τό ποτό του, εἶναι δικό του]
hit: he hit me me kt*ee*peesse [μέ κτύπησε]
hitch-hike oto-stop [ὄτο-στόπ]
   hitch-hiker k*a*nee oto-stop [κάνει ὄτο-στόπ]
hold *(verb)* krat*o* [κρατῶ]
hole ee treepa [ἡ τρύπα]
holiday theeakopes [διακοπές]
   I'm on holiday *ee*me se theeakopes [εἶμαι σέ
   διακοπές] *see* **public**
home to sp*ee*tee [τό σπίτι]
   I want to go home *the*lo na p*a*o speetee [θέλω
   νά πάω σπίτι]
   at home sto speetee [στό σπίτι]
   homesick nostalg*o* to sp*ee*tee moo [νοσταλγῶ
   τό σπίτι μου]
honest t*ee*meeos [τίμιος]
   honestly? l*o*go teem*ee*s? [λόγω τιμῆς;]
honey to m*e*lee [τό μέλι]
   honeymoon o m*ee*nas too m*e*leetos [ὁ μήνας
   τοῦ μέλιτος]

hope ee elp*ee*tha [ἡ ἐλπίδα]
    I hope that ... elp*ee*zo *o*tee ... [ἐλπίζω ὅτι]
    I hope so/not elp*ee*zo n*e*/okhee [ἐλπίζω
    ναί/ὄχι]
horn *(car)* to kl*a*xon [τό κλάξον]
horrible freekt*o*s [φρικτός]
hors d'oeuvre orekt*ee*ka [ὀρεκτικά]
horse to *a*logo [τό ἄλογο]
hospital to nosokom*ee*o [τό νοσοκομεῖο]
    » *TRAVEL TIP: see* **doctor**
host o eekothesspot*ee*s [ὁ οἰκοδεσπότης]
hostess ee eekoth*e*sspeena [ἡ οἰκοδέσποινα]
    (air) ee aerosseenoth*o*s [ἡ ἀεροσυνοδός]
hot zest*o* [ζεστό]
    (spiced) peek*a*ndeeko [πικάντικο]
hotel to ksenothokh*ee*o [τό ξενοδοχεῖο]
hour ee *o*ra [ἡ ὥρα]
house to sp*ee*tee [τό σπίτι]
    housewife ee eekok*ee*ra [ἡ οἰκοκυρά]
how pos [πῶς]
    how many p*o*ssee [πόσοι]
    how much p*o*ssa [πόσα]
    how often k*a*th*e* pote [κάθε πότε]
    how long p*o*sso ker*o* [πόσο καιρό]
    how long have you been here? p*o*sso ker*o*
    *ee*sste etho? [πόσο καιρο εἶστε ἐδῶ;]
    how are you? tee k*a*nees? [τί κάνεις;]
hull to skar*ee* [τό σκαρί]
humid eegr*o*s [ὑγρός]
humour h*u*mor [χιούμορ]
    haven't you got a sense of humour? then
    *e*khees k*a*th*o*loo h*u*mor? [δέν ἔχεις καθόλου
    χιούμορ;]
hundredweight:
    » *TRAVEL TIP: 1 cwt =50.8 kilos*
hungry: I'm hungry/not hungry peen*a*o/then
    peen*a*o [πεινάω/δέν πεινάω]
hurry: I'm in a hurry vee*a*zome [βιάζομαι]
    please hurry! pe*o* greegora parakal*o*! [πιό
    γρήγορα παρακαλῶ]

....

hurt: it hurts pon*a*ee [πονάει]
   my leg hurts pon*a*ee to pothee moo [πονάει τό
   πόδι μου]
   YOU MAY THEN HEAR...
   *ee*ne theenatos ponos? *is it a sharp pain?*
husband: my husband o sseezeegos moo
   [ὁ σύζυγός μου]
I eg*o* [ἐγώ]
   I am English/a teacher *ee*me
   Anglos/tha*ss*kalos [εἶμαι 'Αγγλος/δάσκαλος]
   I am hot/I'm staying here zest*e*nome/m*e*no
   etho [ζεσταίνομαι/μένω ἐδώ]
ice o pagos [ὁ πάγος]
   ice-cream ena pago*to* [ἕνα παγωτό]
   iced coffee kaf*e* frap*e* [καφέ φραπέ]
   with lots of ice me pol*ee* pago [μέ πολύ πάγο]
identity papers ee taftotees [ἡ ταυτότης]
idiot o vl*a*kas [ὁ βλάκας]
if an [ἄν]
ignition ee m*ee*za [ἡ μίζα]
ill arostos [ἄρρωστος]
   I feel ill *ee*me arostos [εἶμαι ἄρρωστος]
illegal paranomos [παράνομος]
illegible theessanagnosto [δυσανάγνωστο]
illness ee arossteea [ἡ ἀρρώστεια]
immediately amessos [ἀμέσως]
import *(noun)* eess*a*go [εἰσάγω]
important spoothe*o*s [σπουδαῖος]
   it's very important *ee*ne pol*ee* seemandeek*o*
   [εἶναι πολύ σημαντικό]
import duty o f*o*ros eessagogees [ὁ φόρος
   εἰσαγωγῆς]
impossible ath*ee*naton [ἀδύνατον]
impressive endeeposseeak*o* [ἐντυπωσιακό]
improve velte*o*no [βελτιώνω]
   I want to improve my ... *the*lo na
   velte*o*sso ... [θέλω νά βελτιώσω ...]
in sto [στό]
inch m*ee*a *ee*ntssa [μία ἴντσα]
» *TRAVEL TIP: 1 inch = 254 cm*

include pereelamvano [περιλαμβάνω]
   does that include breakfast? afto
   pereelamvanee ke to proeeno? [αὐτό
   περιλαμβάνει καί τό πρωϊνό;]
inclusive seemberee-lamvanomenoo
   [συμπεριλαμβανομένου]
incompetent aneekonos [ἀνίκανος]
inconsiderate apereeskeptos [ἀπερίσκεπτος]
incontinent assotos [ἄσωτος]
incredible ekpleekteekos [ἐκπληκτικός]
indecent aprepees [ἀπρεπής]
independent anexarteetos [ἀνεξάρτητος]
India Intheea ['Ινδία]
Indian Inthos ['Ινδός]
indicator theektees poreeas [δείκτης πορείας]
indigestion theesspepseea [δυσπεψία]
indoors sto speetee [στό σπίτι]
industry ee veeomeekhaneea [ἡ βιομηχανία]
infection ee moleensee [ἡ μόλυνση]
infectious koleeteekos [κολλητικός]
inflation o pleethoreesmos [ὁ πληθωρισμός]
informal anepeesseemos [ἀνεπίσημος]
information pleeroforee-es
   [πληροφορίες]
   **do you have any information in English
   about . . .?** meepos ekhete pleeroforee-es sta
   angleeka ya . . .? [μήπως ἔχετε πληροφορίες στά
   'Αγγλικά γιά . . .;]
   is there an information office? eeparkhee
   grafeeo pleeroforeeon? [ὑπάρχει γραφείο
   πληροφοριῶν;]
inhabitant o kateekos [ὁ κάτοικος]
injection meea enessee [μιά ἔνεση]
injured travmateesmenos [τραυματισμένος]
   he's been injured travmateesteeke
   [τραυματίστηκε]
injury to travma [τό τραῦμα]
innocent atho-os [ἄθῶος]
insect ena zoeefeeo [ἕνα ζωΰφιο]
   insect repellent endomoktono [ἐντομοκτόνο]

inside messa [μέσα]
insist: I insist (on it) epeemeno [ἐπιμένω]
insomnia a-eepneea [ἀϋπνία]
instant coffee nescafe
instead, instead of andee [ἀντί]
   can I have that one instead? boro na ekho
   ekeeno andee aftoo? [μπορῶ νά ἔχω ἐκεῖνο ἀντί
   αὐτοῦ;]
insulating tape monoteekee teneea [μονωτική
   ταινία]
insulation ee monossee [ἡ μόνωση]
insult ee prosvolee [ἡ προσβολή]
insurance ee assfaleea [ἡ ἀσφάλεια]
intelligent ekseepnos [ἔξυπνος]
interesting entheeaferon [ἐνδιαφέρον]
international thee-ethnees [διεθνής]
interpreter thee-ermeeneas [διερμηνέας]
   would you interpret for us? boreete na
   metafrassete ya mas? [μπορεῖτε να μεταφράσετε
   γιά μᾶς;]
into messa [μέσα]
introduce: can I introduce . . . ? boro na sas
   seessteesso . . . ? [μπορῶ νά σᾶς συστήσω . . . ;]
invalid *(noun)* o anapeeros [ὁ ἀνάπηρος]
   invalid chair anapeereekee karekla
   [ἀναπηρική καρέκλα]
invitation proskleessee [πρόσκληση]
   thank you for the invitation efkhareesto ya
   teen proskleessee [εὐχαριστῶ γιά τήν
   πρόσκληση]
invite: can I invite you out? borona sas
   proskalesso na vgoome exo? [μπορῶ νά σᾶς
   προσκαλέσω νά βγοῦμε ἔξω;]
Ireland Irlantheea [᾿Ιρλανδία]
Irish Irlanthos [᾿Ιρλανδός]
iron *(for clothes) (noun)* ena eelektreeko
   seethero [ἕνα ἠλεκτρικό σίδερο]
   will you iron these for me? boreete na moo
   seetherossete afta? [μπορεῖτε νά μοῦ σιδερώσετε
   αὐτά;]

ironmonger's to pseeleekadzeetheeko [τό ψιλικατζίδικο]
» *TRAVEL TIP: typically a general store in Greece (not for food though); will sell books and stamps*
is *ee*ne [εἶναι]
island to neess*ee* [τό νησί]
it aft*o* [αὐτό]
  it is ... *ee*ne ... [εἶναι ...]
Italian Ital*os* ['Ιταλός]
Italy Ital*ee*a ['Ιταλία]
itch fagoor*a* [φαγούρα]
  it itches me tro*ee* [μέ τρώει]
itemize: would you itemize it for me? bor*ee*te na moo to katagrapsete? [μπορεῖτε νά μοῦ τό καταγράψετε;]
jack o gr*ee*los [ὁ γρύλος]
jacket to sak*a*k*ee* [τό σακάκι]
jam to gleek*o* [τό γλυκό]
  traffic jam boteele*a*reesma [μποτιλιάρισμα]
January Eeanoo-*a*reeos ['Ιανουάριος]
jaw to sagon*ee* [τό σαγόνι]
jealous zeelee*a*rees [ζηλιάρης]
jeans jeans [τζήνς]
jellyfish mee*a* ts*oo*khtra [μιά τσούχτρα]
jetty o m*o*los [ὁ μῶλος]
jewellery ta kosm*ee*mata [τά κοσμήματα]
jib flok*os* [φλόκος]
job ee thoolee*a* [ἡ δουλειά]
  just the job aft*o* akr*ee*vos [αὐτό ἀκριβῶς]
joke *(noun)* ast*ee*o [ἀστεῖο]
  you must be joking astee-*e*vesse s*ee*goora [ἀστειεύεσαι σίγουρα]
journey to tax*ee*thee [τό ταξίδι]
  have a good journey kalo tax*ee*thee [καλό ταξίδι]
July Ee-*oo*leeos ['Ιούλιος]
jumper to poolover [τό πουλόβερ]
junction ee thee*a*-sta*v*rossee [ἡ διασταύρωση]
June Ee-*oo*neeos ['Ιούνιος]
junk koorelar*ee*-es [κουρελάριες]

just: just two mono th*ee*o [μόνο δύο]
  just there ek*ee* akreevos [ἐκεῖ ἀκριβῶς]
  not just now okhee tora am*ess*os [ὄχι τώρα
  ἀμέσως]
  just now m*o*lees tora [μόλις τῶρα]; *(a little
  while ago)* preen apo l*ee*go [πρίν ἀπό λίγο]
  that's just right aft*o ee*na otee prepee [αὐτό
  εἶναι ὅτι πρέπει]
keen: I'm very keen to . . . *the*lo polee na . . .
  [θέλω πολύ νά . . .]
  I'm not keen then polee*the*lo [δέν πολυθέλω]
keep: can I keep it? boro na to krat*ee*sso
  [μπορῶ νά τό κρατήσω]
  you keep it p*a*rto ess*ee* [πάρ' το ἐσύ]
  keep the change kr*a*ta ta r*e*ssta [κράτα τά
  ρέστα]
  you didn't keep your promise then
  kr*a*teesses teen eepo-skhess*ee* soo [δέν κράτησες
  τήν ὑπόσχεσή σου]
kettle o vrast*ee*ras [ὁ βραστήρας]
key to kleeth*ee* [τό κλειδί]
kidney to nefr*o* [τό νεφρό]
kill *(verb)* skotono [σκοτώνω]
kilo to kil*o* [τό κιλό]
» TRAVEL TIP: conversion: $\dfrac{kilos}{5} \times 11 = pounds$

kilos	1	1½	5	6	7	8	9
pounds	2.2	3.3	11	13.2	15.4	17.6	19.8

kilometre kheelee*oo*metro [χιλιόμετρο]
» TRAVEL TIP: conversion: $\dfrac{kilometres}{8} \times 5 = miles$

kilometres	1	5	10	20	50	100
miles		0.62	3.11	6.2	12.4	31	62

kind: that's very kind of you aft*o ee*ne polee
  evgeneeko ek m*e*roos sas [αὐτό εἶναι πολύ
  εὐγενικό ἐκ μέρους σας]
kiosk to per*ee*eptero [τό περίπτερο]
» TRAVEL TIP: *at kiosks on the street you can buy
  tobacco, books, chocolate, soft drinks etc; they
  also have telephones and sell stamps*

kiss *(noun)* ena feel*ee* [ἕνα φιλί]
kitchen ee koo*zee*na [ἡ κουζίνα]
knee to gonato [τό γόνατο]
knickers ee keelota [ἡ κυλόττα]
knife ena makher*ee* [ἕνα μαχαίρι]
knock *(verb)* kteepo [κτυπῶ]
　there's a knocking noise from the engine
　ak*oo*gete *e*nas metaleekos *tho*reevos apo *tee*
　meekhan*ee* [ἀκούγετε ἕνας μεταλικός θόρυβος
　ἀπό τή μηχανή]
know ksero [ξέρω]
　I don't know then ksero [δέν ξέρω]
label *(noun)* ee eteeketa [ἡ ἐτικέττα]
laces *(shoe)* korthon*ee*a [κορδόνια]
lacquer ee lak [ἡ λάκ]
ladies *(toilet)* geenekon [γυναικῶν]
lady me*e*a keer*ee*a [μιά κυρία]
lager b*ee*ra [μπύρα]
　lager and lime b*ee*ra me 'lime' [μπύρα μέ λάϊμ]
lamb *(meat)* arn*ee* [ἀρνί]
lamp ee lampa [ἡ λάμπα]
　lampshade ena ambazoor [ἕνα ἀμπαζούρ]
　lamp-post o steelos [ὁ στῦλος]
land *(noun)* ee yee [ἡ γῆ]
lane *(car)* ee loreetha [ἡ λωρίδα]
language glossa [γλῶσσα]
large megalos [μεγάλος]
laryngitis lareeng*ee*tees [λαρυγγίτης]
last teleft*e*os [τελευταῖος]
　last year/week ton perasmeno khrono/teen
　perasmenee evthomatha [τόν περασμένο
　χρόνο/τήν περασμένη ἑβδομάδα]
　last night kh-*the*ss vrathee [χθές βράδυ]
　at last! ep*ee* teloos! [ἐπί τέλους!]
late: sorry I'm late me seen-khor*ee*te poo
　arg*ee*ssa [μέ συγχωρῆτε που ἄργησα]
　it's a bit late *ee*ne kapos arga [εἶναι κάπως
　ἀργά]
　please hurry, I'm late pe*e*o greegora
　parakalo, *e*kho arg*ee*ssee [πιό γρήγορα

παρακαλῶ, ἔχω ἀργήσει]
at the latest to argotero [τό ἀργότερο]
later argotera [ἀργότερα]
   see you later *th*a se tho argotera [θά σέ δῶ ἀργότερα]
latitude to geografeeko platos [τό γεωγραφικό πλάτος]
laugh *(verb)* ye-lo [γελῶ]
launderette to pleendeereeo [τό πλυντήριο]
lavatory ee tooaleta [ἡ τουαλέττα]
law o nomos [ὁ νόμος]
lawyer theekeegoros [δικηγόρος]
laxative katharseeo [καθάρσιο]
lay-by to parking [τό πάρκινγκ]
lazy tembelees [τεμπέλης]
leaf to feelo [τό φύλλο]
leak *(noun)* ee theearoee [ἡ διαρροή]
   it leaks stazee [στάζει]
learn: I want to learn ... *the*lo na matho ... [θέλω νά μάθω . . .]
lease *(verb)* neekeeazo [νοικιάζω]
least: not in the least katholoo [καθόλου]
   at least toolakheesston [τουλάχιστον]
leather therma [δέρμα]
   this meat's like leather afto to kreaseene san sola [αὐτό τό κρέας εἶναι σάν σόλα]
leave: we're leaving tomorrow fevgome avreeo [φεύγομε αὔριο]
   when does the bus leave? pote fevgee to leoforeeo? [πότε φεύγει τό λεωφορεῖο;]
   I left two shirts in my room afeessa theeo pokameessa sto thomateeo moo [ἄφησα δύο πουκάμισα στό δωμάτιο μου]
   can I leave this here? boro nafeesso afto etho? [μπορῶ ν' ἀφήσω αὐτό ἐδῶ;]
left areestera [ἀριστερά]
   on the left pros tareestera [πρός τ' ἀριστερά]
   left-handed areesteros [ἀριστερός]
» *TRAVEL TIP: the word for 'left-handed' in Greek also means 'communist'*

left luggage (office) khoros felaxeos aposkevon [χῶρος φυλάξεως ἀποσκευῶν]
leg to pothee [τό πόδι]
legal nomeemos [νόμιμος]
lemon ena lemonee [ἔνα λεμόνι]
lemonade meea lemonatha [μιά λεμονάδα]
lend: will you lend me your . . .? borees na moo thaneessees . . .? [μπορεῖς νά μοῦ δανείσεις . . .;]
lengthen makreno [μακραίνω]
lens o fakos [ὁ φακός]
Lent ee sarakostee [ἡ Σαρακοστή]
less leegoteros [λιγότερος]
   less than that leegotero apo ekeeno [λιγότερο ἀπ᾽ ἐκεῖνο]
let: let me help asse me na voeetheeso [ἄσε με νά βοηθήσω]
   let me go! asse me na feego! [ἄσε με νά φύγω!]
   will you let me off here? borees na me afeessees na katevo etho? [μπορεῖς νά μέ ἀφήσεις νά κατέβω ἐδῶ;]
   let's go pame [πᾶμε]
letter to grama [τό γράμμα]
   are there any letters for me? ekho kanena grama? [ἔχω κανένα γράμμα;]
   letterbox takheethromeeko kootee [ταχυδρομικό κουτί]
lettuce to maroolee [τό μαρούλι]
level-crossing eessopethe theeavassee [ἰσόπεδη διάβαση]
liable *(responsible)* eepeftheenos [ὑπεύθυνος]
library ee veevleeotheekee [ἡ βιβλιοθήκη]
licence ee atheea [ἡ ἄδεια]
lid to kapakee [τό καπάκι]
lie *(noun)* ena psema [ἔνα ψέμα]
   can he lie down for a bit? boree na ksaplossee ya leego? [μπορεῖ νά ξαπλώσει γιά λίγο;]
life ee zoee [ἡ ζωή]
   life assurance asfaleea zoees [ἀσφάλεια ζωῆς]
   lifebelt, life jacket to sosseeveeo [τό σωσίβιο]

lifeboat ee sos*see*veeos le*m*vos [ἡ σωσίβιος λέμβος]

life-guard o navagoss*o*stees [ὁ ναυαγοσώστης]

lift: do you want a lift? *the*lete na sas p*a*o? [θέλετε νά σᾶς πάω;]

could you give me a lift? bor*ee*te na me p*a*te? [μπορεῖτε νά μέ πάτε;]

the lift isn't working o anelkees*tee*ras then thoo*le*vee [ὁ ἀνελκυστήρας δέν δουλεύει]

light: the lights aren't working ta f*o*ta then an*a*voon [τά φῶτα δέν ἀνάβουν]

have you got a light? *e*khete fote*a*? [ἔχετε φωτιά;]

when it gets light *o*tan kseemer*o*ssee [ὅταν ξημερώσει]

light bulb l*a*mpa [λάμπα]

light meter fot*o*metro [φωτόμετρο]

(not heavy) elafr*o*s [ἐλαφρός]

like: would you like . . .? *th*a *the*late . . .? [θά θέλατε . . .;]

I'd like a . . ./I'd like to . . . *th*a *ee*th*e*la ena . . ./*th*a*eeth*ela na . . . [θά εἴθελα ἕνα . . ./θά εἴθελα νά . . .]

I like it/you moo ar*e*ssee/moo ar*e*ssees [μοῦ ἀρέσει/μοῦ ἀρέσεις]

I don't like it then moo ar*e*ssee [δέν μοῦ ἀρέσει]

what's it like? me tee mee*a*zee? [μέ τί μοιάζει;]

do it like this k*a*ne to *e*tssee [κάνε το ἔτσι]

lime 'lime' [λάιμ]

line gram*ee* [γραμμή]

lip to kh*ee*lee [τό χείλι]

lip salve voot*ee*ro kak*a*o [βούτυρο κακάο]

lipstick kokeen*a*thee [κοκκινάδι]

liqueur ena l*ee*ker [ἕνα λικέρ]

list *(noun)* o kat*a*logos [ὁ κατάλογος]

listen ak*oo*-o [ἀκούω]

litre ena l*ee*tro [ἕνα λίτρο]

» *TRAVEL TIP: 1 litre = 1½ pints = 0.22 gals*

little meekros [μικρός]
  a little ice/a little more leego pago/akomee
  leego [λίγο πάγο/ἀκόμη λίγο]
  just a little mono leego [μόνο λίγο]
live zo [ζῶ] **I live in Glasgow** meno stee
  Glasskovee [μένω στή Γλασκώβη]
  where do you live? poo menees? [ποῦ μένεις;]
liver to seekotee [τό συκώτι]
lizard ee savra [ή σαύρα]
loaf meea frandzola [μιά φραντζόλα]
lobster o astakos [ὁ ἀστακός]
local: could we try a local wine? boroome na
  thokeemassome to dopeeo krassee? [μπορούμε
  νά δοκιμάσομε τό ντόπιο κρασί;]
  a local restaurant ena esteeatoreeo tees
  pereeokhees [ἕνα ἐστιατόριο τῆς περιοχῆς]
lock: the lock's broken ee kleethareea eene
  spasmenee [ἡ κλειδαριά εἶναι σπασμένη]
  I've locked myself out kleethotheeka exo
  [κλειδώθηκα ἔξω]
lonely monakheekos [μοναχικός]
long makrees [μακρής]
  we'd like to stay longer tha thelame na
  mename pereessotero [θά θέλαμε νά μέναμε
  περισσότερο]
  that was long ago afto eetane preen apo polee
  kero [αὐτό ἤτανε πρίν ἀπό πολύ καιρό]
longitude geografeeko meekos [γεωγραφικό
  μῆκος]
loo: where's the loo? pooeene ee tooaleta? [ποῦ
  εἶναι ἡ τουαλέττα;]
look: you look tired fenesse koorasmenos
  [φαίνεσαι κουρασμένος]
  I'm looking forward to . . . pereemeno me
  aneepomoneesseea na . . . [περιμένω μέ
  ἀνυπομονησία νά . . .]
  I'm looking for . . . psakhno ya . . . [ψάχνω
  γιά . . .]
  look out! prossekhe! [πρόσεχε!]
loose khalaros [χαλαρός]

lorry to forteego [τό φορτηγό]
    lorry driver otheegos forteegoo [ὁδηγός
    φορτηγοῦ]
lose khano [χάνω]
    I've lost my bag ekhassa teen tsanta moo
    [ἔχασα τήν τσάντα μου]
    excuse me, I'm lost me seen-khoreete, ekho
    khathee [μέ συγχωρεῖτε, ἔχω χαθεῖ]
lost property apolesthenda [ἀπολεσθέντα]
lot: a lot/not a lot pola/okhee pola [πολλά/ὄχι
    πολλά]
    a lot of chips/wine poles patates
    teeganeetes/polee krassee [πολλές πατάτες
    τηγανιτές/πολύ κρασί]
    a lot more expensive polee peeo akreevo
    [πολύ πιό ἀκριβό]
    lots pola [πολλά]
lotion ee losseeon [ἡ λοσιόν]
loud theenata [δυνατά]
    louder peeo theenata [πιό δυνατά]
love: I love you sagapo [σ' ἀγαπῶ]
    do you love me? magapas? [μ' ἀγαπᾶς;]
    he's in love eene erotevmenos [εἶναι
    ἐρωτευμένος]
    I love this wine maressee afto to krassee
    [μ' ἀρέσει αὐτό τό κρασί]
lovely oreos [ὡραῖος]
low khameelos [χαμηλός]
luck ee teekhee [ἡ τύχη]
    good luck! kalee teekhee! [καλή τύχη!]
lucky teekheros [τυχερός]
    you're lucky eesse teekheros [εἶσαι τυχερός]
    that's lucky afto eene teekhero
    [αὐτό εἶναι τυχερό]
luggage ee aposkeves [οἱ ἀποσκεύες]
lumbago to loombako [τό λουμπάκο]
lump to preexeemo [τό πρήξιμο]
lunch to ye-vma [τό γεῦμα]
lung o pnevmonas [ὁ πνεύμωνας]
luxurious poleetelees [πολυτελής]

luxury poleeteleeas [πολυτελείας]
mad trelos [τρελλός]
madam keereea [κυρία]
made-to-measure rameno kata parangeleea
  [ραμένο κατά παραγγελία]
magazine to pereeotheeko [τό περιοδικό]
magnificent magaloprepees [μεγαλοπρεπής]
maiden name patroneemo [πατρώνυμο]
mail gramata [γράμματα]
mainland sto essotereeko tees khoras [στό
  ἐσωτερικό τῆς χώρας]
main road o kendreekos thromos [ὁ κεντρικός
  δρόμος]
make kano [κάνω]
  will we make it in time? tha prolavome? [θά
  προλάβομε;]
  make-up to make-up [τό μέϊκ ἄπ]
man o anthras [ὁ ἄνδρας]
manager o theeakheereestees [ὁ διαχειριστής]
  can I see the manager? boro na tho ton
  deeakheereestee? [μπορῶ νά δῶ τόν
  διαχειρηστή;]
manicure maneekeeoor [μανικιούρ]
manners ee tropee [οἱ τρόποι]
many polee [πολλοί]
map o khartees [ὁ χάρτης]
  a map of Athens ena khartee tees Atheenas
  [ἕνα χάρτη τῆς ᾿Αθήνας]
March Marteeos [Μάρτιος]
margarine ee margareenee [ἡ μαργαρίνη]
marina ee provleeta [ἡ προβλήτα]
mark: there's a mark on it ekhee ena
  seemathee [ἔχει ἕνα σημάδι]
market, marketplace ee agora [ἡ ἀγορά]
marmalade ee marmelatha [ἡ μαρμελάδα]
married pandremenos [πανδρεμένος]
marry: will you marry me? tha me
  pandreftees? [θά μέ πανδρευτεῖς;]
marvellous thavmasseeos [θαυμάσιος]
mascara ee maskara [ἡ μασκάρα]

mashed potatoes pata*tes* poor*e* [πατάτες πουρέ]
massage 'massage' [μασάζ]
mast to kat*artee* [τό κατάρτι]
mat khal*akee* [χαλάκι]
match *e*na sp*eerto* [ἕνα σπίρτο]
  a box of matches *e*na koot*ee* sp*eerta* [ἕνα
  κουτί σπίρτα]
  football match pothossfereek*os* agonas
  [ποδοσφαιρικός ἀγώνας]
material eeleek*o* [ὑλικό]
matter: it doesn't matter then peer*azee* [δέν
  πειράζει]
  what's the matter? tee seemb*enee*? [τί
  συμβαίνει;]
mattress to stroma [τό στρῶμα]
mature *o*reemos [ὥριμος]
maximum m*e*geestos [μέγιστος]
May Ma*e*eos [Μάϊος]
may: may I have . . .? th*a* boroossa na*e*kho . . .?
  [θά μπορούσα νά ἔχω . . .;]
maybe bor*ee* [μπορεῖ]
mayonnaise mageeon*e*za [μαγιονέζα]
me ego [ἐγώ]
  can you hear me? makoos? [μ' ἀκοῦς;]
  please give it to me se parak*alo* thosse moo to
  [σέ παρακαλῶ δῶσε μου τό]
meal ye-vma [γεῦμα]
mean: what does this mean? tee eno*ee* afto?
  [τί ἐννοεῖ αὐτό;]
measles eelara [ἰλαρά]
  German measles ereethr*a* [ἐρυθρά]
measurements m*e*tra [μέτρα]
meat to kr*eas* [τό κρέας]
mechanic: is there a mechanic here?
  eep*arkhee* kan*e*nas meekhaneek*os* eth*o*?
  [ὑπάρχει κανένας μηχανικός ἐδῶ;]
medicine to farmako [τό φάρμακο]
meet seenand*o* [συναντῶ]
  pleased to meet you kh*e*rome poo sas
  gnor*eez*o [χαίρομαι πού σᾶς γνωρίζω]

....

when can we meet again? pote boro na se
ksanatho? [πότε μπορῶ νά σέ ξαναδῶ;]
meeting seenandeesee [συνάντηση]
melon peponee [πεπόνι]
member melos [μέλος]
   how do I become a member? pos boro na
   geeno melos? [πῶς μπορῶ νά γίνω μέλος;]
men ee anthres [οἱ ἄνδρες]
mend: can you mend this? boreete na
epeeskevassete afto? [μπορεῖτε νά ἐπισκευάσετε
αὐτό;]
mention: don't mention it parakalo
[παρακαλῶ]
menu katalogos fageeton [κατάλογος φαγητῶν]
   can I have the menu, please? boro na ekho
   ton katalogo, parakalo? [μπορῶ νά ἔχω τόν
   κατάλογο, παρακαλῶ;] *see pages 69–71*
mess anakatoma [ἀνακάτωμα]
message: are there any messages for me?
eeparkhee kanena meeneema ya mena?
[ὑπάρχει κανένα μήνυμα γιά μένα;]
   can I leave a message for . . .? boro nafeesso
   ena meeneema ya . . .? [μπορῶ ν' ἀφήσω ἕνα
   μήνυμα γιά . . .;]
metre to metro [τό μέτρο]
» *TRAVEL TIP: 1 metre = 39.37 ins = 1.09 yds*
midday messeemeree [μεσημέρι]
middle messo [μέσο]
   in the middle stee messee [στή μέση]
midnight messaneekta [μεσάνυκτα]
might: I might be late boree nargeesso [μπορεῖ
ν' ἀργήσω]; **he might have gone** boree
nakhee feegee [μπορεῖ νἄχει φύγει]
migraine eemeekraneea [ἡμικρανία]
mild eepeeos [ἤπιος]
mile ena meelee [ἕνα μίλι]

» *TRAVEL TIP: conversion:* $\dfrac{miles}{5} \times 8 = kilometres$

miles	½	1	3	5	10	50	100
kilometres	0.8	1.6	4.8	8	16	80	160

ΟΡΕΚΤΙΚΑ   OREKTEEKA   APPETISERS

Ντολμαδάκια Dolmadakia
vine leaves stuffed with minced meat, rice and herbs

Μελιτζανοσαλάτα Melitzanosalata
eggplant salad

Κεφτέδες Keftedes
meat balls

Ταραμοσαλάτα Taramosalata
fish roe pâté

Σπανακόπιτα Spanakopita
spinach squares

Χταπόδι Khtapothee
boiled octopus

Σαγανάκι Saganaki
fried cheese and egg

Σαλάτα χωριάτικη Salata khoreeateekee
mixed salad

Κολοκυθάκια τηγανιτά Kolokeethakeea teeganeeta
fried baby marrows

Κοκορέτσι Kokoretsi
spit-roasted liver and innards

Τζατζίκι Tzantziki
*a mixture of cucumber, yogurt and garlic –
sounds awful but worth a try!*

ΣΟΥΠΕΣ   SOOPES   SOUPS

Αὐγολέμονο Avgolemono
chicken broth, lemon and egg

Κακαβιά Kakavia
various kinds of fish

Πατσάς Patzas
intestines of lamb thoroughly washed and cut up

Φασολάδα Fassolatha
hot bean soup

Μαγειρήτσα Magiritsa
traditional lamb soup served on the Saturday night before Easter Sunday

Ψαρόσουπα   Pssarossoopa
fish soup

MAIN DISHES

Στιφάδο   Stifado
hare or rabbit stew with onions
Μουσακᾱ   Moussaka
*layers of either eggplant or potatoes, minced
meat topped with thick creamy sauce and baked*
Γιουβαρλάκια   Yiouvarlakia
minced meat, rice and seasoning in sauce
Παστίτσιο   Pastichio
macaroni, minced meat and thick creamy sauce
Γιουβέτσι   Yiouvetsi
roast lamb with pasta
'Αρνί φρικασέ   Arni frikasse
lamb, lettuce and thick white sauce
'Αγκινάρες   Agginares
artichokes in light sauce
Τομάτες γεμιστές   Domates yemeestes
tomatoes with a stuffing of mince, rice and herbs
Πιπεριές γεμιστές   Peeperee-es yemeestes
stuffed green peppers
Γαριδοπίλαφο   Gareethopeelafo
prawns with rice cooked in butter
Λαχανοντολμάδες   Lakhanodolmathes
cabbage leaves stuffed with rice and mince

ΘΑΛΑΣΣΙΝΑ   THALASSINA   SEAFOOD

Μπακαλιάρος   Bakaliaros
cod, fried or boiled
'Αστακός   Asstakos
lobster, grilled or boiled
Γαρίδες   Gareethes
prawns, grilled or boiled
Καλαμαράκια   Kalamarakeea
fried baby squid
Καβούρια   Kavoureea
boiled crab

Μύδια Meetheea
  mussels

ΤΥΡΙΑ	TEEREEA	CHEESES

Μανούρι Manouri
  hard cheese
Φέτα Feta
  soft white cheese
Κασέρι Kasseri
  mild yellow cheese
Κεφαλοτύρι Kefalotiri
  hard cheese, very salty
Άνθότυρο Anthotiro
  aromatic cheese
Don't expect each cheese to be always consistent in
  taste

ΓΛΥΚΑ	GLEEKA	SWEETS

Γαλακτομπούρεκο Galatoboureko
  thin pastry with custard filling
Καταΐφι Kataifi
  shredded pastry with nuts and honey
Κουραμπιέδες Kourabiethes
  Greek shortbread
Μελομακάρονα Melomakarona
  fritters coated in nuts and syrup
Άμυγδαλοτά Amigthalota
  almond pastries
Βανίλια Vanillia
  vanilla-flavoured sweet or ice-cream
Πορτοκάλι Portokalee
  orange, boiled and sugared
Μπακλαβάς Baklavas
  pastry filled with nuts and syrup
Βύσσινο Veesseeno
  cherries, boiled and sugared
Λουκουμάδες Lookoomathes
  fritters coated in honey
Παγωτό Pagoto
  ice cream

milk ga la [γάλα]
 a glass of milk ena poteeree ga la [ἕνα ποτήρι γάλα]
 milkshake milkshake [μίλκσέϊκ]
millimetre kheelee-osto [χιλιοστό]
milometer to konter [τό κοντέρ]
minced meat o keemas [ὁ κιμᾶς]
mind: I've changed my mind a laxa gnomee [ἄλαξα γνώμη]
 I don't mind then me enokhlee [δέν μέ ἐνοχλεῖ]
 do you mind if I ...? th a se peeraze an ...? [θά σέ πείραζε ἄν ...;]
 never mind then peerazee [δέν πειράζει]
mine theeko moo [δικό μου]
mineral water metaleeko nero [μεταλλικό νερό]
minimum ela kheestos [ἐλάχιστος]
minus pleen [πλήν]
minute lepto [λεπτό]
 in a minute se ena lepto [σέ ἕνα λεπτό]
 just a minute ena lepto [ἕνα λεπτό]
mirror o kathreftees [ὁ καθρέπτης]
Miss thespeenees [Δεσποινῆς]
miss: I miss you moo leepees [μοῦ λείπεις]
 he's missing leepee [λείπει]
 there is a ... missing leepee ena ... [λείπει ἕνα ...]
mist omeekhlee [ὀμίχλη]
mistake lathos [λάθος]
 I think you've made a mistake nomeezo otee ekhees ka nee ena lathos [νομίζω ὅτι ἔχεις κάνει ἕνα λάθος]
misunderstanding parexeegeessee [παρεξήγηση]
modern moderno [μοντέρνο]
Monday Theftera [Δευτέρα]
money lefta [λεφτά]
 I've lost my money ekhassa ta lefta moo [ἔχασα τά λεφτά μου]
month meenas [μῆνας]
moon to fegaree [τό φεγγάρι]

moorings to angeerovoleeo [τό ἀγκυροβόλιο]
moped to meekhanakee [τό μηχανάκι]
more pereessotero [περισσότερο]
   can I have some more? boro na ekho akomee
   leego? [μπορῶ νά ἔχω ἀκόμη λίγο;]
   more wine, please kee alo krassee parakalo
   [κι᾽ ἄλλο κρασί, παρακαλῶ]
   no more ftanee [φτάνει]
   more comfortable peeo anapafteekee [πιό
   ἀναπαυτική]
   more than pereessotero apo [περισσότερο
   ἀπό]
morning proee [πρωΐ]
   good morning kaleemera [καλημέρα]
   in the morning to proee [τό πρωΐ]
   this morning afto to proee [αὐτό τό πρωΐ]
most: I like it the most moo aressee peeo polee
   apo ola [μοῦ ἀρέσει πιό πολύ ἀπό ὅλα]
   most of the time/the people seeneethos/ee
   pereessoteree anthropee [συνήθως/οἱ
   περισσότεροι ἄνθρωποι]
mosquito ena koonoopee [ἕνα κουνούπι]
motel motel [Μοτέλ]
mother: my mother ee meetera moo [ἡ μητέρα
   μου]
motor ee meekhanee [ἡ μηχανή]
motorbike to motossako [τό μοτοσακό]
motorboat varka me meekhanee [βάρκα μέ
   μηχανή]
motorcyclist motosseekleteestees
   [μοτοσυκλετιστής]
motorist otheegos aftokeeneetoo [ὁδηγός
   αὐτοκινήτου]
motorway ethneekee othos [ἐθνική ὁδός]
mountain to voono [τό βουνό]
mouse ena pondeekee [ἕνα ποντίκι]
moustache moostakee [μουστάκι]
mouth to stoma [τό στόμα]
   mouth-watering lee-onee sto stoma [λυώνει
   στό στόμα]

move: don't move mee koonee-*e*sse [μή
κουνιέσαι]
   could you move your car? bor*ee*te na
metakeen*ee*ssete to aftok*ee*neeto sas? [μπορεῖτε
νά μετακινήσετε τό αὐτοκίνητό σας;]
Mr K*ee*reeos [Κος]
Mrs Keer*ee*a [Κα]
Ms *no Greek equivalent*
much pol*ee* [πολύ]
   much better/much more pol*ee* kal*ee*tera/
per*ee*ss*o*tera [πολύ καλλίτερα/περισσότερα]
   not much *o*khee pol*ee* [ὄχι πολύ]
mug: I've been mugged me l*ee*stepsan [μέ
λήστεψαν]
mum mamm*a* [μαμμά]
muscle o mees [ὁ μῦς]
museum to moos*ee*eo [τό μουσεῖο]
mushroom to maneet*a*ree [τό μανιτάρι]
music moos*ee*k*ee* [μουσική]
must: I must have ... pr*e*pee na *e*kho ...
[πρέπει νά ἔχω . . .]
   I must not eat ... then prepee na f*a*-o ... [δέν
πρέπει νά φάω . . .]
   you must pr*e*pee [πρέπει]
   must I? pr*e*pee? [πρέπει;]
mustard moos*ta*rtha [μουστάρδα]
my moo [μοῦ]; **my hotel** to ksenothok*ee*o moo
[τό ξενοδοχεῖο μου]
nail *(finger)* to n*ee*khee [τό νύχι]
   (wood) to karf*ee* [τό καρφί]
   nailfile mee*a* l*ee*ma neekhee-*o*n [μιά λίμα
νυχιῶν]
   nail polish man*o* [μανό]
   nail clippers o neekhok*o*ptees [ὁ νυχοκόπτης]
   nail scissors ena psal*ee*thee ya n*ee*kheea [ἕνα
ψαλίδι γιά νύχια]
naked geemn*o*s [γυμνός]
name *o*noma [ὄνομα]
   my name is ... me l*e*ne ... [μέ λένε . . .]
   what's your name? pos se l*e*ne? [πῶς σέ λένε;]

napkin petsseta [πετσέτα]
nappy pana [πάνα]
narrow steno [στενό]
national ethneekos [ἐθνικός]
nationality ethneekotees [ἐθνικότης]
natural feesseekos [φυσικός]
naughty: don't be naughty meen eesse
ataktos [μήν εἶσαι ἄτακτος]
near: is it near? eene konda? [εἶναι κοντά;]
near here etho konda [ἐδῶ κοντά]
do you go near . . .? pas konda . . .? [πᾶς
κοντά . . .;]
where's the nearest . . .? poo eene to
pleessee-estero . . .? [πού εἶναι τό
πλησιέστερο . . .;]
nearly skhethon [σχεδόν]
neat (drink) sketo [σκέτο]
necessary anangeo [ἀναγκαῖο]
it's not necessary then khreeazete [δέν
χρειάζεται]
neck o lemos [ὁ λαιμός]
necklace to kolee-e [τό κολλιέ]
need: I need a . . . khreeazome ena . . .
[χρειάζομαι ἕνα . . .]
needle meea velona [μιά βελόνα]
neighbour o yee-tonas [ὁ γείτονας]
neither: neither of them kanenas apo toos
theeo [κανένας ἀπό τούς δύο]
neither . . . nor . . . oote . . . oote
[οὔτε . . . οὔτε]
neither do I oote kee ego [οὔτε κι' ἐγώ]
nephew: my nephew o anepseeos moo
[ὁ ἀνεψιός μου]
nervous taragmenos [ταραγμένος]
net (fishing) to theektee [τό δίκτυ]
(hair) o feeles [ὁ φιλές]
net price katharee teemee [καθαρή τιμή]
never pote [ποτέ]
well I never! okhee pote! [ὄχι ποτέ!]
new neo [νέο]

....

New Year Neo etos [Νέο ἔτος]
New Year's Eve Paramonee tees
Protokhroneeas [Παραμονή τῆς Πρωτοχρονιᾶς]
Happy New Year kharoomenee
protokhroneea [Χαρούμενη Πρωτοχρονιά]
» *TRAVEL TIP: the lights are turned out at
midnight; after midnight it's a Greek custom to
play cards*
news ta nea [τά νέα]
  newsagent o efeemereethopolees [ὁ
  ἐφημεριδοπώλης]
  newspaper ee efeemereetha [ἡ ἐφημερίδα]
  do you have any English newspapers?
  ekhete Angleekes efeemereethes?
  [ἔχετε Ἀγγλικές ἐφημερίδες;]
New Zealand Nea Zeelantheea [Νέα Ζηλανδία]
New Zealander Neo Zeelanthos [Νεο Ζηλανδός]
next o epomenos [ὁ ἐπόμενος]
  sit next to me katsse konda moo [κάτσε κοντά
  μου]
  please stop at the next corner parakalo
  stamateeste steen epomenee strofee [παρακαλῶ
  σταματῆστε στήν ἐπόμενη στροφή]
  see you next year tha se tho too khronoo [θά
  σέ δῶ τοῦ χρόνου]
  next week/next Tuesday teen alee
  evthomatha/Treetee [τήν ἄλλη ἑβδομάδα/Τρίτη]
nice kalo [καλό]
niece: my niece ee aneepseea moo [ἡ ἀνηψιά
  μου]
night vrathee [βράδυ]
  good night kaleeneekta [καληνύκτα]
  at night to vrathee [τό βράδυ]
  night porter neektereenos theeroros
  [νυκτερινός θυρωρός]
  is there a good night club here? ekhee
  kanena kalo night club etho? [ἔχει κανένα καλό
  νάϊτ κλάμπ ἐδῶ;]
  night-life neektereenee zoee [νυκτερινή ζωή]
no okhee [ὄχι]

there's no water then ekhee nero [δέν ἔχει νερό]

no way! apoklee-ete [ἀποκλείεται]

I've no money then ekho lefta [δέν ἔχω λεφτά]

» *TRAVEL TIP: rolling the head upwards and back means 'no' in Greece*

nobody kanenas [κανένας]

  nobody saw it kanenas then to eethe [κανένας δέν τό εἶδε]

noisy thoreevothees [θορυβώδης]

  our room is too noisy to thomateeo mas ekhee polee fassareea [τό δωμάτιό μας ἔχει πολύ φασαρία]

none kanees [κανείς]

  none of them kanenas ap aftoos [κανένας ἀπ' αὐτούς]

nonsense anoeessee-es [ἀνοησίες]

normal feesseeologeekos [φυσιολογικός]

north o voras [ὁ βορράς]

Northern Ireland Vorios Irlantheea [Βόρειος Ἰρλανδία]

nose ee meetee [ἡ μύτη]

  nosebleed emorageea apo tee meetee [αἱμοραγία ἀπό τή μύτη]

not then [δέν]

  I'm not hungry then peenao [δέν πεινάω]

  not that one okhee afto [ὄχι αὐτό]

  not me/you okhee ego/essee [ὄχι ἐγώ/ἐσύ]

  not here/there okhee etho/ekee [ὄχι ἐδῶ/ἐκεῖ]

  I do not want to then thelo [δέν θέλω]

  he didn't tell me then moo eepe [δέν μου εἶπε]

note *(bank note)* khartonomeesma [χαρτονόμισμα]

nothing teepote [τίποτε]

November Noemvreeos [Νοέμβριος]

now tora [τώρα]

nowhere poothena [πουθενά]

nudist geemneesstees [γυμνιστής]

  nudist beach paraleea geemneeston [παραλία γυμνιστῶν]

nuisance: it's a nuisance *ee*ne bel*a*s [εἶναι μπελᾶς]
  this man's being a nuisance *ee*ne enokhleeteekos [εἶναι ἐνοχλητικός]
numb mootheeasm*e*nos [μουδιασμένος]
number aree*th*mos [ἀριθμός]
  number plate peenak*ee*thes [πινακῖδες]
nurse nossokomos [νοσοκόμος]
nut to kar*ee*thee [τό καρύδι]
  (for bolt) ena paxeem*a*thee [ἕνα παξιμάδι]
oar to koop*ee* [τό κουπί]
obligatory eepokhreoteek*a* [ὑποχρεωτικά]
obviously profan*o*s [προφανῶς]
occasionally kam*ee*a for*a* [καμιά φορά]
occupied kateeleem*e*nee [κατειλημμένη]
  is this seat occupied? *ee*ne kateeleem*e*nee aft*ee* ee *the*ssee? [εἶναι κατειλημμένη αὐτή ἡ θέση;]
o'clock *see* **time**
October Okt*o*vreeos [᾿Οκτώβριος]
octopus khtapothee [χταπόδι]
odd *(number)* mon*o*s [μονός]
  (strange) par*a*xenos [παράξενος]
of too [τοῦ]
off: the milk/meat is off to g*a*la/kr*e*as kh*a*lasse [τό γάλα/κρέας χάλασε]
  it just came off m*o*lees vg*ee*ke [μόλις βγῆκε]
  10% off th*e*ka tees ekat*o* *e*kptossee [10% ἔκπτωση]
offence prosvol*ee* [προσβολή]
office grafe*ee*o [γραφεῖο]
officer *(to policeman)* keeree-e assteenome [κύριε ἀστυνόμε]
official *(noun)* epe*e*sseemos [ἐπίσημος]
often seekhn*a* [συχνά]
  not often okhee seekhn*a* [ὄχι συχνά]
oil l*a*thee [λάδι]
  will you change the oil? bor*ee*te nal*a*xete ta l*a*thee*a*? [μπορεῖτε ν' ἀλλάξετε τά λάδια;]
ointment aleef*ee* [ἀλοιφή]
OK end*a*xee [ἐντάξει]

old ye-ros [γέρος]
    how old are you? posso khronon eese? [πόσο
    χρονῶν εἶσαι;]
    I am 25 eeme 25 khronon [εἶμαι 25 χρονῶν]
olive ee eleea [ἡ ἐληά]
    olive oil eleolatho [ἐλεόλαδο]
omelette omeleta [ὀμελέττα]
on pano [πάνω]
    I haven't got it on me then toekho mazee moo
    [δέν τό ἔχω μαζί μου]
    on Friday teen Paraskevee [τήν Παρασκευή]
    on television steen teeleorassee [στήν
    τηλεόραση]
once meea fora [μιά φορά]
    at once amessos [ἀμέσως]
one enas [ἕνας]
    the red one to kokeeno [τό κόκκινο]
onion ena kremeethee [ἕνα κρεμύδι]
only mono [μόνο]
open (adjective) aneekta [ἀνοικτά]
    I can't open it then boro na to aneexo [δέν
    μπορῶ νά τό ἀνοίξω]; **when do you
    open?** pote aneegete? [πότε ἀνοίγετε;]
opera ee opera [ἡ ὄπερα]
operation engkheereessee [ἐγχείρηση]
    will I need an operation? tha khreeassto
    engkheereessee? [θά χρειαστῶ ἐγχείρηση;]
operator (telephone) o teelefoneetees [ὁ
    τηλεφωνητής]
opposite apenandee [ἀπέναντι]
    opposite the hotel apenandee apo to
    ksenothokheeo [ἀπέναντι ἀπό τό ξενοδοχεῖο]
optician o opteekos [ὁ ὀπτικός]
or ee [ἤ]
orange portokalee [πορτοκάλι]
    orange juice kheemos portokaleeoo [χυμός
    πορτοκαλιοῦ]
order: could we order now? boroome na
    parangeelome tora? [μπορούμε νά
    παραγγείλωμε τώρα;]

thank you, we've already ordered
efkhareest*o e*khome *ee*thee parang*ee*lee
[εὐχαριστῶ ἔχομε ἤδη παραγγείλει]
other: the other one to *a*lo [τό ἄλλο]
do you have any others? *e*khete t*ee*pote *a*la?
[ἔχετε τίποτε ἄλλα;]
otherwise theeaforeteek*a* [διαφορετικά]
ought: I ought to go pr*e*pee na f*ee*go [πρέπει νά
φύγω]
ounce oog*ee*a [οὐγγιά]
» *TRAVEL TIP: 1 ounce = 28.35 grammes*
our: our hotel to ksenothokh*ee*o mas [τό
ξενοδοχεῖο μας]; **that's ours** afto *ee*ne theeko
mas [αὐτό εἶναι δικό μας]
out: we're out of petrol m*ee*name ap*o*
venz*ee*nee [μείναμε ἀπό βενζίνη]
get out! v-yes *e*xo! [βγές ἔξω!]
outboard exol*e*mveeos [ἐξωλέμβιος]
outdoors *e*xo [ἔξω]
outside: can we sit outside? bor*oo*me na
kath*ee*ssoome *e*xo? [μποροῦμε νά καθίσουμε
ἔξω;]
over: over here/there etho/ekee [ἐδῶ/ἐκεῖ]
over 40 p*a*no ap*o* sar*a*nda [πάνω ἀπό 40]
it's all over ol*a* tel*ee*ossan [ὅλα τελείωσαν]
overboard: man overboard! *a*nthropos stee
*tha*lassa [ἄνθρωπος στή θάλασσα]
overcharge: you've overcharged me me
khr*e*ossate parap*a*no [μέ χρεώσατε παραπάνω]
overcooked parapseem*e*no [παραψημένο]
overexposed para-ektethe*e*m*e*no
[παραεκτεθιμένο]
overnight *(stay, travel)* theeaneekt*e*refssee
[διανυκτέρευση]
oversleep parakeem*a*me [παρακοιμᾶμαι]
I overslept parakeem*ee*theeka
[παρακοιμήθηκα]
overtake prosp*e*rno [προσπερνῶ]
owe: what do I owe you? p*o*ssa sas khrosst*a*o?
[πόσα σᾶς χρωστάω;]

own: my own ... theek*o* moo [δικό μου]
  are you on your own? *ee*sse m*o*nos soo? [εἶσαι
  μόνος σου;]; **I'm on my own** *ee*me m*o*nos moo
  [εἶμαι μόνος μου]
owner o eetheeokt*ee*tees [ὁ ἰδιοκτήτης]
oxygen to oxeegono [τό ὀξυγόνο]
oyster to stree*thee* [τό στρείδι]
pack: I haven't packed yet then *e*kana tees
  val*ee*ts*e*s moo ak*o*ma [δέν ἔκανα τίς βαλίτσες
  μου ἀκόμα]
  can I have a packed lunch? bor*oo*me na
  p*a*roome paketar*ee*sm*e*no fag*ee*to? [μπροροῦμε
  νά πάρουμε πακεταρισμένο φαγητό;]
package tour omatheek*ee* ekthrom*ee* [ὁμαδική
  ἐκδρομή]
page *(of book)* ee sel*ee*tha [ἡ σελίδα]
  could you page him? bor*ee*ete na ton fon*a*xete
  apo to megafono? [μπορεῖτε νά τόν φωνάξετε
  ἀπό τό μεγάφωνο;]
pain o ponos [ὁ πόνος]
  I've got a pain in my chest *e*kho ena pono sto
  stee*th*os moo [ἔχω ἕνα πόνο στό στῆθος μου]
  pain-killers pafss*ee*pona [παυσίπονα]
painting ee zografeek*ee* [ἡ ζωγραφική]
Pakistan Pakees*tan* [Πακιστάν]
Pakistani Pakeestan*os* [Πακιστανός]
pale khlom*os* [χλωμός]
pancake teegan*ee*ta [τηγανίτα]
panties ee keel*o*tes [οἱ κυλόττες]
pants pantalon*ee*a [παντελόνια]
  (underpants) to sleep*a*kee [τό σλιπάκι]
paper khart*ee* [χαρτί]
  (newspaper) efeemer*ee*tha [ἐφημερίδα]
parcel ena pak*e*to [ἕνα πακέτο]
pardon? *(didn't understand)* seegno*mee*?
  [συγγνώμη;]
  I beg your pardon *(sorry)* me seenkhor*ee*te
  [μέ συγχωρεῖτε]
parents: my parents ee gon*ee*s moo [οἱ γονεῖς
  μου]

park to parko [τό πάρκο]
  where can I park my car? poo boro na
  parkaro to aftokeeneeto moo? [πού μπορῶ νά
  παρκάρω τό αὐτοκίνητό μου;]
part meros [μέρος]
partner o seeneteros [ὁ συνέταιρος]
party *(group)* ee omatha [ἡ ὁμάδα]
  (celebration) to partee [τό πάρτυ]
  I'm with the ... party eeme me teen ...
  omatha [εἶμαι μέ τήν . . . ὁμάδα]
pass *(mountain)* perasma [πέρασμα]
  he's passed out leepotheemeesse
  [λιποθύμησε]
passable *(road)* theeavatos [διαβατός]
passenger o epeevatees [ὁ ἐπιβάτης]
passer-by o theeavatees [ὁ διαβάτης]
passport to theeavateereeo [τό διαβατήριο]
past: in the past sto parelthon [στό παρελθόν]
  see **time**
pastry zeemee [ζύμη]
  (cake) gleekeesma [γλύκισμα]
path to monopatee [τό μονοπάτι]
patient: be patient kane eepomonee [κάνε
  ὑπομονή]
pattern skhetheeo [σχέδιο]
pavement to pezothromeeo [τό πεζοδρόμιο]
pay pleerono [πληρώνω]
  can I pay, please? boro na pleerosso
  parakalo? [μπορῶ νά πληρώσω παρακαλῶ;]
  » *TRAVEL TIP: you normally pay when you leave not
  when you order your drinks etc*
peace eereenee [Εἰρήνη]
peach ena rothakeeno [ἕνα ροδάκινο]
peanuts feessteekeea arapeeka [φυστίκια
  ἀράπικα]
pear ena akhlathee [ἕνα ἀχλάδι]
peas beezeleea [μπιζέλια]
pebble khaleekee [χαλίκι]
pedal to peethalee [τό πηδάλι]
pedestrian o pezos [ὁ πεζός]

pedestrian crossing thee*a*vasse pez*o*n
[διάβαση πεζών]
» *TRAVEL TIP: don't assume that cars will always
stop for you!*
peg *e*na mandal*a*kee [ἕνα μαντaλάκι]
pelvis ee lek*a*nee [ἡ λεκάνη]
pen *e*na steel*o* [ἕνα στυλό]
  have you got a pen? *e*khete *e*na steel*o*? [ἔχετε
  ἕνα στυλό;]
pencil *e*na mol*ee*vee [ἕνα μολύβι]
penfriend f*ee*los thee aleelografee*e*as [φίλος δι'
  ἀλληλογραφίας]
penicillin peneekeel*ee*nee [πενικιλλίνη]
penknife o soogee*a*s [ὁ σουγιάς]
pensioner seendaxee*oo*khos [συνταξιοῦχος]
people *a*nthropee [ἄνθρωποι]
  the Greek people o Eleeneek*o*s laos
  [ὁ Ἑλληνικός λαός]
pepper to peep*e*ree [τό πιπέρι]
  (vegetable) me*e*a peepere*e*a [μιά πιπεριά]
peppermint m*e*nta [μέντα]
per: per night/week/person to vrathee/teen
  evthom*a*tha/to *a*tomo [τό βράδυ/τήν
  ἑβδομάδα/τό ἄτομο]
per cent tees ekat*o* [τοῖς ἑκατό]
perfect t*e*leeos [τέλειος]
  the perfect holiday ee eethaneek*e*s
  theeakop*e*s [οἱ ἰδανικές διακοπές]
perfume *a*roma [ἄρωμα]
perhaps *ee*ssos [ἴσως]
period *(also medical)* pereeothos [περίοδος]
perm permana*n*t [περμανάντ]
permit *(noun)* atheea [ἄδεια]
person *a*tomo [ἄτομο]
  in person prossopeeka [προσωπικά]
petrol venz*ee*nee [βενζίνη]
  petrol station venz*ee*nee [βενζίνη]
» *TRAVEL TIP: ap*lee ['ἁπλή] *is 2 star;* so*uper
  [σούπερ] *is 3 or 4 star*
philosopher *e*nas feel*o*ssofos [ἕνας φιλόσοφος]

photograph meea fotografeea [μιά φωτογραφία]
  would you take a photograph of us? boreete
  na mas vgalete meea fotografeea? [μπορεῖτε νά
  μᾶς βγάλετε μιά φωτογραφία;]
piano peeano [πιάνο]
pickpocket enas portofolas [ἕνας πορτοφολάς]
picture meea eekona [μιά εἰκόνα]
pie peeta [πίτα]
piece ena komatee [ἕνα κομμάτι]
  a piece of . . . ena komatee apo . . . [ἕνα
  κομμάτι ἀπό . . .]
pig ena gooroonee [ἕνα γουρούνι]
pigeon ena pereesteree [ἕνα περιστέρι]
pile-up karabola [καραμπόλα]
pill to khapee [τό χάπι]
  do you take the pill? pernees to khapee?
  [παίρνεις τό χάπι;]
pillion ee sela [ἡ σέλλα]
  on the pillion pano stee sela [πάνω στή σέλλα]
pillow ena maxeelaree [ἕνα μαξιλάρι]
pin meea karfeetssa [μιά καρφίτσα]
pineapple enas ananas [ἕνας ἀνανάς]
pint meea peenta [μιά πίντα]
» TRAVEL TIP: 1 pint = 0.57 litres
pink roz [ρόζ]
pipe ee peepa [ἡ πίπα]
  pipe tobacco kapnos peepas [καπνός πίπας]
piston to peesstonee [τό πιστόνι]
pity: it's a pity eene kreema [εἶναι κρῖμα]
place meros [μέρος]
  is this place taken? eene peeasmenee aftee ee
  thessee? [εἶναι πιασμένη αὐτή ἡ θέση;]
  do you know any good places to go? kserete
  teepote kala meree na pao? [ξέρετε τίποτε καλά
  μέρη νά πάω;]
plain (not patterned) okhee garneereesmeno [ὄχι
  γαρνιρισμένο]
  plain food aplo fageeto [ἁπλό φαγητό]
plane to a-eroplano [τό ἀεροπλάνο]
  by plane a-eroporeekos [ἀεροπορικῶς]

plant to feet*o* [τό φυτό]
plaster *(medical)* o yee-pssos [ὁ γύψος]
  see **sticking**
plastic plasteek*o* [πλαστικό]
plate *e*na pee*a*to [ἕνα πιάτο]
platform platf*o*rma [πλατφόρμα]
  which platform please? pee*a* platf*o*rma
  parakal*o*? [ποιά πλατφόρμα παρακαλῶ;]
pleasant efkh*a*reestos [εὐχάριστος]
please: could you please . . .? parakal*o*,
  bor*ee*te . . .? [παρακαλῶ, μπορεῖτε . . .;]
  (yes) please ne parakal*o* [ναί παρακαλῶ]
pleasure efkhar*ee*ssteessee [εὐχαρίστηση]
  it's a pleasure khar*a* mas [χαρά μας]
plenty: plenty of . . . pol*a* ap*o* . . . [πολλά
  ἀπό . . .]
  thank you, that's plenty efkhar*ee*sto aft*o*
  *ee*ne arket*o* [εὐχαριστῶ αὐτό εἶναι ἀρκετό]
pliers m*ee*a penssa [μιά πένσα]
plonk *(wine)* kak*ee*s pee*o*teetas krass*ee* [κακής
  ποιότητας κρασί]
plug *(electrical)* ee preeza [ἡ πρίζα]
  (car) to booz*ee* [τό μπουζί]
  (sink) tapa [τάπα]
plum *e*na tham*a*skeeno [ἕνα δαμάσκηνο]
plumber eethravleek*o*s [ὑδραυλικός]
plus seen [σύν]
p.m. meta mess*ee*mvre*e*a [μ.μ. μετά
  μεσημβρία]
pneumonia pnevmon*ee*a [πνευμονία]
poached egg avg*o* poss*e* [αὐγό ποσέ]
pocket ee ts*e*pee [ἡ τσέπη]
point: could you point to it? bor*ee*te na to
  th*ee*xete? [μπορεῖτε νά τό δείξετε;]
  four point six t*e*ssera k*o*ma ex*ee* [τέσσερα
  κόμα ἔξι]
  points *(car)* plat*ee*nes [πλατίνες]
police ee asst*ee*n*o*me*e*a [ἡ ἀστυνομία]
  get the police eethope*e*-e*e*ste teen
  asst*ee*nom*e*a [εἰδοποιήστε τήν ἀστυνομία]

policeman assteenomeekos [ἀστυνομικός]
police station to assteenomeeko tmeema [τό
ἀστυνομικό τμῆμα]
» *TRAVEL TIP: dial 100*
polish *(noun)* verneekee [βερνίκι]
will you polish my shoes? boreete na
ya-leessete ta papootsseea moo? [μπορεῖτε νά
γυαλίσετε τά παπούτσια μου;]
polite evgeneekos [εὐγενικός]
politics poleeteeka [πολιτικά]
polluted moleesmeno [μολυσμένο]
polythene bag meea na-eelon sakoola [μιά
νάϋλον σακούλα]
pool *(swimming)* ee peesseena [ἡ πισίνα]
poor: I'm very poor eeme polee ftokhos [εἶμαι
πολύ φτωχός]
poor quality kakee peeotees [κακή ποιότης]
popular theemofeelees [δημοφιλής]
population o pleetheesmos [ὁ πληθυσμός]
pork kheereeno [χοιρινό]
port to leemanee [τό λιμάνι]
(drink) port [πόρτ]
to port areessteree plevra too pleeoo [ἀριστερή
πλευρά τοῦ πλοίου]
porter o akh-thoforos [ὁ ἀχθοφόρος]
portrait to portreto [τό πορτρέτο]
posh poleetelees [πολυτελής]
possible peethano [πιθανό]
could you possibly . . .? tha sas eetan
theenaton na . . .? [θά σᾶς ἦταν δυνατό νά . . .;]
post takheethromo [ταχυδρομῶ]
postcard ee karta [ἡ κάρτα]
post office to takheethromeeo [τό
ταχυδρομεῖο]
» *TRAVEL TIP: letter boxes are yellow; stamps can
also be bought at tobacconists, kiosks and
sometimes ironmongers*
poste resante post restand
[πόστ-ρεστάντ]
potato ee patata [ἡ πατάτα]

pottery kerameek*a* [κεραμικά]
pound ee leetra [ή λίτρα]
  (money) ee leera [ή λίρα]

» *TRAVEL TIP: conversion:* $\dfrac{pounds}{11} \times 5 = kilos$

pounds	1	3	5	6	7	8	9
kilos	0.45	1.4	2.3	2.7	3.2	3.6	4.1

pour: it's pouring vrekhe pol*ee* [βρέχει πολύ]
powder ee poothra [ή πούδρα]
power cut theeakop*ee* revmatos [διακοπή
  ρεύματος]
power point ee preeza [ή πρίζα]
prawns gareethes [γαρίδες]
prefer: I prefer this one proteem*o* aft*o*
  [προτιμώ αὐτό]
pregnant engheeos [ἔγκυος]
prescription mee*a* seentag*ee* [μιά συνταγή]
present: at present pros to paron [πρός τό
  παρόν]
  here's a present for you aft*o* ee*ne* ena thoro
  ya sena [αὐτό εἶναι ἕνα δῶρο γιά σένα]
president o pro-ethros [ὁ πρόεδρος]
press: could you press these? boree*te* na
  seetheross*e*te afta? [μπορεῖτε νά σιδερώσετε
  αὐτά;]
pretty *o*rea [ὡραία]
  pretty good pol*ee* kalo [πολύ καλό]
price ee teem*ee* [ή τιμή]
priest o pap*as* [ὁ παππάς]
printed matter teepomeno eeleek*o* [τυπωμένο
  ὑλικό]
prison ee feelak*ee* [ή φυλακή]
private eetheeoteek*os* [ἰδιωτικός]
probably pee*th*anos [πιθανῶς]
problem ena provleema [ἕνα πρόβλημα]
product pro-ee-*o*n [προϊόν]
profit to kerthos [τό κέρδος]
promise: do you promise? eeposkhesse?
  [ὑπόσχεσαι;]
  I promise eeposkhome [ὑπόσχομαι]

pronounce: how do you pronounce this? pos
to proferees afto? [πῶς τό προφέρεις αὐτό;]
propeller ee propela [ἡ προπέλλα]
properly opos prepee [ὅπως πρέπει]
property eetheeokteesseea [ἰδιοκτησία]
prostitute ee pornee [ἡ πόρνη]
protect prosstatevo [προστατεύω]
Protestant Protestandees [Προτεστάντης]
proud eepereefanos [ὑπερήφανος]
prove: I can prove it boro na to apotheexo
[μπορῶ νά τό ἀποδείξω]
public: the public to keeno [τό κοινό]
  public convenience theemosseea tooaleta
  [δημόσια τουαλέττα]
» TRAVEL TIP: *public conveniences are extremely*
  few and far between; but it's quite usual to use
  the toilet in bars, cafes, restaurants, hotels
  without asking
» TRAVEL TIP: *Public Holidays*
  1 January Protokhroneea
  [Πρωτοχρονιά] *New Year's Day*
  6 January Theofaneea [Θεοφάνεια] *Epiphany*
  25 March Ethneekee Eortee [Ἐθνική
  Ἑορτή] *National Day*
  Megalee Paraskevee [Μεγάλη
  Παρασκευή] *Good Friday*
  Megalo Savato [Μεγάλο Σάββατο] *Easter*
  Saturday
  Paskha [Πάσχα] *Easter*
  1 May Ergateekee eortee [Ἐργατική
  Ἑορτή] *Labour Day*
  15 August Keemeessee tees Theotokoo
  [Κοίμηση τῆς Θεοτόκου] *Assumption*
  28 October Ethneekee eortee [Ἐθνική
  Ἑορτή] *National Day*
  25 December Khreestoogena
  [Χριστούγεννα] *Christmas*
  26 December Seenaxee Theotokoo [Σύναξη
  Θεοτόκου] *Boxing Day*
pudding pooteengha [πουτίγγα]

pull *(verb)* travo [τραβῶ]
he pulled out in front of me petakhteeke
brosta moo [πετάχτηκε μπροστά μου]
pump ee andleea [ἡ ἀντλία]
punctual: he is very punctual eene panda
steen ora too [εἶναι πάντα στήν ὥρα του]
puncture meea treepa sto lasteekho [μιά τρύπα
στό λάστιχο]
pure agnos [ἀγνός]
purple mov [μώβ]
purse to portofolee [τό πορτοφόλι]
push *(verb)* sprokhno [σπρώχνω]
don't push mee sprokhnees [μή σπρώχνεις]
push-chair karotssakee [καροτσάκι]
put: where can I put ...? poo boro na valo ...?
[ποῦ μπορῶ νά βάλω ...;]
pyjamas ee peetzames [οἱ πυτζάμες]
quality ee peeotees [ἡ ποιότης]
quarantine ee karanteena [ἡ καραντίνα]
quarter ena tetarto [ἕνα τέταρτο]
a quarter of an hour ena tetarto teesoras [ἕνα
τέταρτο τῆς ὥρας]
quay ee provleeta [ἡ προβλήτα]
question meea eroteessee [μιά ἐρώτηση]
queue *(noun)* ee oora [ἡ οὐρά]
» *TRAVEL TIP: orderly queuing is not so widespread
as in the UK*
quick greegora [γρήγορα]; **that was quick** afto
eetan greegoro [αὐτό ἦταν γρήγορο]
quiet eesseekha [ἥσυχα]
be quiet! seeopee! [σιωπή!]
quite endelos [ἐντελῶς]
(fairly) arketa [ἀρκετά]
quite a lot pola [πολλά]
radiator *(car)* pseegeeo aftokeeneetoo [ψυγεῖο
αὐτοκινήτου]
(heater) to kaloreefer [τό καλοριφέρ]
radio to ratheeofono [τό ραδιόφωνο]
rail: by rail seetheerothromeekos
[σιδηροδρομικῶς]

....

rain ee vrok*hee* [ή βροχή]
  it's raining vr*e*khee [βρέχει]
  raincoat ee kabard*ee*na [ή καμπαρντίνα]
rally *(car)* r*a*lee [ράλυ]
rape veeasmos [βιασμός]
rare sp*a*neeos [σπάνιος]
  (steak) okhee pol*ee* pseem*e*no [όχι πολύ ψημένο]
raspberry vat*o*mooro [βατόμουρο]
rat *e*nas aroor*e*os [ένας άρουραίος]
rather: I'd rather sit here protee*mo* na
  kath*ee*sso eth*o* [προτιμῶ νά καθήσω ἐδῶ]
  I'd rather not then *that*hela [δέν θἄθελα]
  it's rather hot *ee*ne m*a*lon zesto [εἶναι μάλλον
  ζεστό]
raw om*o* [ώμό]
razor kseer*a*fee [ξυράφι]
  razor blades kseeraf*a*keea [ξυραφάκια]
read: you read it thee*a*vaze to ess*ee* [διάβαζέ το
  ἐσύ]
  something to read k*a*tee na theeav*a*sso [κάτι
  νά διαβάσω]
ready: when will it be ready? pote *th*a *ee*ne
  eteem*o*? [πότε θά εἶναι ἕτοιμο;]
  I'm not ready yet then *ee*me eteemos˙ ak*o*mee
  [δέν εἶμαι ἕτοιμος ἀκόμη]
real pragmateek*o*s [πραγματικός]
really pragmateek*a* [πραγματικά]
rear-view mirror kath*re*ftees aftokeen*ee*too
  [καθρέφτης αὐτοκινήτου]
reasonable logeek*o*s [λογικός]
receipt apoth*ee*xee [ἀπόδειξη]
  can I have a receipt, please? bor*ee*te na moo
  thossete m*ee*a apoth*ee*xee, p*a*rakalo? [μπορείτε
  νά μου δώσετε μία ἀπόδειξη, παρακαλῶ;]
recently prossf*a*ta [πρόσφατα]
reception *(hotel)* ee ressepsee*o*n [ή ρεσεψιόν]
  at reception stee ressepsee*o*n [στήν ρεσεψιόν]
receptionist ee ressepsseeon*ee*st
  [ή ρεσεψιονίστ]
recipe ee seendag*ee* [ή συνταγή]

recommend: can you recommend ...?
boreete na moo seessteessete ...? [μπορεῖτε
νά μοῦ συστήσετε ...;]
record *(music)* o theeskos [ὁ δίσκος]
red kokkeeno [κόκκινο]
reduction *(in price)* ekptossee [ἔκπτωση]
refuse: I refuse arnoome [ἀρνοῦμαι]
region ee pereefereea [ἡ περιφέρεια]
in this region saftee teen pereefereea [σ' αὐτή
τήν περιφέρεια]
registered letter seesteemeno grama
[συστημένο γράμμα]
regret leepoome [λυποῦμαι]
I have no regrets then metaneeossa katholoo
[δέν μετάνοιωσα καθόλου]
relax: I just want to relax thelo na eeremeesso
mono [θέλω νά ἠρεμήσω μόνο]
relax! eeremeesse! [ἠρέμησε!]
remember: don't you remember? then
theemassee? [δέν θυμᾶσαι;]
I'll always remember tha theemame panda
[θά θυμᾶμαι πάντα]
something to remember you by katee geea
na se theemame [κάτι γιά νά σέ θυμᾶμαι]
rent: can I rent a car/boat/bicycle? boro na
neekeeasso ena aftokeeneeto/meea varka/ena
potheelato? [μπορῶ νά νοικιάσω ἕνα
αὐτοκίνητο/μιά βάρκα/ἕνα ποδήλατο;]
repair: can you repair it? boreete na to
epeeskevassete? [μπορεῖτε νά τό ἐπισκευάσετε;]
repeat: could you repeat that? boreete na to
epanalavete? [μπορεῖτε νά τό ἐπαναλάβετε;]
reputation ee feemee [ἡ φήμη]
rescue *(verb)* sozo [σώζω]
reservation krateessee thesseos [κράτηση
θέσεως]
I want to make a reservation for ... thelo na
krateesso thessees geea ... [θέλω νά κρατήσω
θέσεις γιά ...]
reserve: can I reserve a seat? boro na kleesso

mee*a the*ssee? [μπορῶ νά κλείσω μιά θέση;]

responsible eep*efth*eenos [ὑπεύθυνος]

rest: I've come here for a rest *ee*rtha etho gee*a* na ksekoorasto [ἤρθα ἐδῶ γιά νά ξεκουραστῶ]
you keep the rest kratee*ste ta eepo*leepa [κρατῆστε τά ὑπόλοιπα]

restaurant to esteeat*oreeo* [τό ἐστιατόριο]

retired seendaxee*oo*khos [συνταξιοῦχος]

return: a return/two returns to . . . me epeestrofee/thee*o* me epeestrof*ee* [μέ ἐπιστροφή/δύο μέ ἐπιστροφή]

reverse gear *o*peess*th*en [ὄπισθεν]

rheumatism revmatees*mee* [ρευματισμοί]

Rhodes Rothos [Ρόδος]

rib ee plevra [ἡ πλευρά]

rice reezee [ρύζι]

rich *(person, food)* ploos*see*os [πλούσιος]

ridiculous ye-leeos [γελεῖος]

right: that's right sossta [σωστά]
you're right ekhees the*ekee*o [ἔχεις δίκιο]
on the right sta thexee*a* [στά δεξιά]
right now t*o*ra am*e*ssos [τώρα ἀμέσως]
right here etho [ἐδῶ]
righthand drive me thexee*o* teem*o*nee [μέ δεξιό τιμόνι]

ring *(on finger)* to thaktee*lee*thee [τό δακτυλίδι]

ripe *o*reemos [ὥριμος]

rip-off: it's a rip-off *ee*ne leess*tee*a [εἶναι ληστεία]

river to pota*mee* [τό ποτάμι]

road o thromos [ὁ δρόμος]
which is the road to . . .? pee*os ee*ne o thromos pros . . .? [ποιός εἶναι ὁ δρόμος πρός . . .;]
roadhog adzam*ees* othee*g*os [ἀτζαμής ὁδηγός]

rob: I've been robbed me lee*stepsan [μέ λήστευσαν]

rock o br*æ*khos [ὁ βράχος]
whisky on the rocks whisky me pag*a*kee*a* [οὐίσκι μέ παγάκια]

roll *(bread)* ena psom*a*kee [ἕνα ψωμάκι]
Roman Catholic K*a*th*o*leekos [Καθολικός]
romantic romandeekos [ρομαντικός]
roof ee orof*ee* [ἡ ὀροφή]
room to thom*a*teeo [τό δωμάτιο]
  have you got a (single/double) room?
  ekhete ena mono/thep*l*o thom*a*teeo? [ἔχετε ἕνα
  μονό/διπλό δωμάτιο;]
  for one night/for three nights gee*a* m*ee*a
  vrath*ee*a/gee*a* tr*ee*s vrathee-*es* [γιά μιά
  βραδιά/γιά τρεῖς βραδιές]
  YOU MAY THEN HEAR . . .
  then *e*khome *we're full up*
  me b*a*neeo ee me khor*ee*s b*a*neeo? *with bath or*
  without bath?
  *e*khome mono gee*a* . . . brath*ee*-*es only*
  for . . . *nights*
room service s*e*rvees thomat*ee*oo [σέρβις
  δωματίου]
rope to skh*ee*n*ee* [τό σχοινί]
rose to treeand*a*feelo [τό τριαντάφυλο]
rough *(person)* agr*ee*kos [ἀγροῖκος]
  (sea) treekeem*ee*othess [τρικυμιώδης]
roughly *(approximately)* p*a*no k*a*to [πάνω κάτω]
roulette rool*e*ta [ρουλέττα]
round *(circular)* strogh*ee*los [στρογγυλός]
roundabout plat*ee*a [πλατεία]
» TRAVEL TIP: *be careful, ca*r*s on a roundabout*
  don't have priority
route por*ee*a [πορεία]
  which is the prettiest/fastest route? pee*o*s
  *ee*ne pee*o* or*e*os/pee*o* s*ee*ndomos thro*m*os? [ποιός
  εἶναι ποιό ὡραῖος/ποιό σύντομος δρόμος;]
rowing boat m*ee*a v*a*rka me koopee*a* [μιά βάρκα
  μέ κουπιά]
rubber l*a*ssteekho [λάστιχο]
  rubberband ena lasstekh*a*kee [ἕνα
  λαστιχάκι]
rubbish *(garbage)* skoopeeth*ee*a [σκουπίδια]
  rubbish! tr*ee*khes! [τρίχες!]

rucksack o sakos [ὁ σάκος]
rudder to peethalee [τό πηδάλι]
rude ageneees [ἀγενής]
ruin ereepeeo [ἐρείπιο]
rum roomee [ρούμι]
    rum and coke roomee me koka-kola [ρούμι μέ κόκα-κόλα]
run: hurry, run! veeassoo, trexe [βιάσου, τρέξε]
    I've run out of petrol/money emeena apo venzeenee/lefta [ἔμεινα ἀπό βενζίνη/λεφτά]
sad leepeemenos [λυπημένος]
safe asfales [ἀσφαλές]
    will it be safe here? thaeene asfales etho? [θά εἶναι ἀσφαλές ἐδῶ;]
    is it safe to swim here? eene asfales na koleembeesome etho? [εἶναι ἀσφαλές νά κολυμπήσωμε ἐδῶ;]
safety asfaleea [ἀσφάλεια]
    safety pin meea paramana [μιά παραμάνα]
sail (verb) taxeethevo me pleeo [ταξιδεύω μέ πλοῖο]
    can we go sailing? boroome na pame varkatha? [μπορούμε νά πᾶμε βαρκάδα;]
sailor naftees [ναύτης]
salad meea salata [μιά σαλάτα]
salami salamee [σαλάμι]
sale: is it for sale? eene ya pooleema? [εἶναι γιά πούλημα;]
salmon o solomos [ὁ σολομός]
salt to alatee [τό ἁλάτι]
same eetheeos [ἴδιος]
    the same again, please to eetheeo ksana parakalo [τό ἴδιο ξανά παρακαλῶ]
    the same to you epeessees [ἐπίσης]
sand ee amos [ἡ ἄμμος]
sandal to santhalo [τό σάνδαλο]
sandwich ena sandwich [ἕνα σάντουϊτς]
sanitary towel servee-etes [σερβιέτες]
satisfactory eekanopee-eeteekos [ἱκανοποιητικός]

Saturday Savato [Σάββατο]
sauce saltssa [σάλτσα]
  saucepan meea katsarola [μιά κατσαρόλα]
saucer ena pee-atakee [ἕνα πιατάκι]
sauna ee saoona [ἡ σάουνα]
sausage ena lookaneeko [ἕνα λουκάνικο]
save *(life)* sozo [σώζω]
say: how do you say . . . in Greek? pos
  lene . . . sta eleeneeka? [πῶς λένε . . . στά
  Ἑλληνικά;]
  what did he say? tee eepe? [τί εἶπε;]
scarf ee sarpa [ἡ σάρπα]
scenery ee thea [ἡ θέα]
schedule to programa [τό πρόγραμμα]
  on/behind schedule steen ora too/ekhee
  katheestereessee [στήν ὥρα του/ἔχει
  καθυστέρηση]
  scheduled flight programateesmenee
  pteessee [προγραματισμένη πτήση]
school to skholeeo [τό σχολεῖο]
scissors: a pair of scissors ena psaleethee [ἕνα
  ψαλίδι]
scooter to skooter [τό σκοῦτερ]
Scotland Skoteea [Σκωτία]
Scottish Skotsezos [Σκωτσέζος]
scratch *(noun)* meea tsagrooneea [μιά
  τσαγκρουνιά]
scream *(verb)* ksefoneezo [ξεφωνίζω]
screw *(noun)* ee veetha [ἡ βίδα]
  screwdriver ena katssaveethee [ἕνα
  κατσαβίδι]
sea ee thalassa [ἡ θάλασσα]
  by the sea konta stee thalassa [κοντά στή
  θάλασσα]
seafood thalasseena [θαλασσινά]
search *(verb)* psakhno [ψάχνω]
  search party omatha erevnees [ὁμάδα
  ἔρευνας]
seasick: I get seasick anakatevome
  [ἀνακατεύομε]

....

I feel seasick ess*tha*nome naft*ee*a [αἰσθάνομαι ναυτία]

seaside paral*ee*a [παραλία]

let's go to the seaside p*a*me stee paral*ee*a [πᾶμε στή παραλία]

season epokh*ee* [ἐποχή]

in the high/low season teen per*ee*odo ekhm*ee*s/nekr*ee* per*ee*odo [τήν περίοδο αἰχμής/νεκρή περίοδο]

seasoning bakhar*ee*k*a* [μπαχαρικά]

seat me*ea the*ssee [μιά θέση]

is this somebody's seat? *ee*ne peeasm*e*nee aft*ee* ee *the*ssee? [εἶναι πιασμένη αὐτή ἡ θέση;]

seat belt z*o*nee assfal*ee*as [ζώνη ἀσφαλείας]

sea-urchin *e*nas akh*ee*nos [ἕνας ἀχινός]

seaweed to f*ee*kee [τό φύκι]

second *(adjective)* th*e*fteros [δεύτερος]

(time) *e*na th*e*fter*o*lepto [ἕνα δευτερόλεπτο]

just a second me*ea* steegm*ee* [μιά στιγμή]

second hand th*e*ftero kh*e*ree [δεύτερο χέρι]

see vlepo [βλέπω]

oh, I see ah, kat*a*lava [ἄ, κατάλαβα]

have you seen . . .? *ee*thate . . .? [εἴδατε . . .;]

can I see the room? boro na th*o* to thom*a*teeo? [μπορῶ νά δῶ τό δωμάτειο;]

seem: it seems so *e*tssee f*e*nete [ἔτσι φαίνεται]

seldom span*ee*a [σπάνια]

self-service s*e*lf-s*e*rvees [σέλφ-σέρβις]

sell pool*o* [πουλῶ]

send st*e*lno [στέλνω]

sensitive evess*th*eetos [εὐαίσθητος]

sentimental ess*th*eemateek*o*s [αἰσθηματικός]

separate *(adjective)* khoreest*o*s [χωριστός]

I'm separated *ee*me se thee*a*sstas*ee* [εἶμαι σέ διάσταση]

can we pay separately? bor*oo*me na pleero*ssoo*me khor*ee*sst*a*? [μπορούμε νά πληρώσυμε χωριστά;]

September Sept*e*mvr*ee*os [Σεπτέμβριος]

serious sovar*o*s [σοβαρός]

I'm serious to leo sovara [τό λέω σοβαρά]
this is serious afto eene sovaro [αὐτό εἶναι
σοβαρό]
is it serious, doctor? eene sovaro, ya-tre?
[εἶναι σοβαρό, γιατρέ;]
service: the service was excellent/poor to
servees eetan exokho/khaleea [τό σέρβις ἦταν
ἔξοχο/χάλια]
  service station venzeenee [βενζίνη]
serviette meea petsseta fageetoo [μιά πετσέτα
φαγητοῦ]
several mereekee [μερικοί]
sexy sexy [σέξυ]
shade: in the shade stee skeea [στή σκιά]
shake koono [κουνῶ]
  to shake hands kheerapsseea [χειραψία]
» TRAVEL TIP: customary to shake hands when you
  meet someone and when you leave them
shallow reekhos [ρηχός]
shame: what a shame! tee kreema! [τί κρῖμα!]
shampoo to sampooan [τό σαμπουάν]
shandy beera me lemonatha [μπύρα μέ
λεμονάδα]
» TRAVEL TIP: a strange thing to ask for; don't
  expect it to taste like real shandy
share (room, table) meerazome [μοιράζομαι]
shark karkhareeas [καρχαρίας]
sharp koftero [κοφτερό]
shave kseereezo [ξυρίζω]
  shaver kseereesteekee meekhanee [ξυριστική
μηχανή]
  shaving foam krema kseereesmatos [κρέμα
ξυρίσματος]
  shaving point preeza kseereesteekees [πρίζα
ξυριστικῆς]
she aftee [αὐτή]
  she is eene [εἶναι]
  she has left efeege [ἔφυγε]
sheep ena arnee [ἕνα ἀρνί]
sheet to sendonee [τό σεντόνι]
shelf to rafee [τό ράφι]

shell to ke**leefos** [τό κέλυφος]
  shellfish *(plural)* ostrako-eeth**ee**
  [ὀστρακοειδῆ]
shelter to katafee**geeo** [τό καταφύγιο]
  can we shelter here? bor**oo**me na
  profeelakht**oo**me eth**o**? [μπορούμε νά
  προφυλαχτοῦμε ἐδῶ;]
sherry ena she**rry** [ἕνα σέρρυ]
ship to pl**eeo** [τό πλοῖο]
shirt to pooka**meesso** [τό πουκάμισο]
shock sok [σόκ]
  I got an electric shock from the . . .
  me teenaxe to revma too . . . [μέ τίναξε τό ρεῦμα
  τοῦ . . .]
  shock-absorber to amortees**ser** [τό
  ἀμορτισέρ]
shoe to papoots**see** [τό παπούτσι]
» *TRAVEL TIP: shoe sizes*

UK	4	5	6	7	8	9	10	11
Greece	37	38	39	41	42	43	44	46

shop to maga**zee** [τό μαγαζί]
  I've some shopping to do ekho na kano
  mereeka psoneea [ἔχω νά κάνω μερικά
  ψώνια]
shore ee akt**ee** [ἡ ἀκτή]
short kond**os** [κοντός]
  I'm three short moo lee**poon** treea [μοῦ
  λείπουν τρία . . .]
  short cut seendomos thromos [σύντομος
  δρόμος]
shorts shorts [σόρτς]
shoulder omos [ὦμος]
shout fona**zo** [φωνάζω]
show: please show me parakalo th**eexe** moo
  [παρακαλῶ δεῖξε μου]
shower: with shower me doos [μέ ντούς]
shrimps gareethes [γαρίδες]
shut: it was shut eetan klees**to** [ἦταν κλειστό]
  when do you shut? pote klee**nete**? [πότε
  κλείνετε;]

shut up! ska*sse!* [σκάσε!]
shy dropal*os* [ντροπαλός]
sick *a*rosst*os* [ἄρρωστος]
  I feel sick anaka*te*vome [ἀνακατεύομαι]
  he's been sick *e*kane emet*o* [ἔκανε ἐμετό]
side plev*ra* [πλευρά]
  side light *f*ota por*ee*as [φῶτα πορείας]
  side street throma*kee* [δρομάκι]
  by the side of the road steen *a*kree too
  thro*moo* [στήν ἄκρη τοῦ δρόμου]
sight: out of sight then *f*enete [δέν φαίνεται]
  the sights ta axee*othe*ata [τά ἀξιοθέατα]
  sightseeing tour ekthrom*ee* sta axee*othe*ata
  [ἐκδρομή στά ἀξιοθέατα]
  we'd like to go on a sightseeing tour
  *the*lome na pa*me* mee*a* ekthrom*ee* na tho*o*me ta
  axee*othe*ata [θέλομε νά πᾶμε μιά ἐκδρομή νά
  δοῦμε τά ἀξιοθέατα]
sign *(notice)* ee peenakee*tha* [ἡ πινακίδα]
signal: he didn't signal then *e*kane s*ee*ma [δέν
  ἔκανε σῆμα]
signature mee*a* eepogra*fee* [μιά ὑπογραφή]
silence seeo*pee* [σιωπή]
silencer ee exa*t*meessee [ἡ ἐξάτμηση]
silk meta*x*ee [μετάξι]
silly an*oe*etos [ἀνόητος]
silver asseem*e*neeos [ἀσημένιος]
similar *o*mee*o*s [ὅμοιος]
simple apl*o* [ἀπλό]
since: since last week apo teen perasm*e*nee
  evthoma*tha* [ἀπό τήν περασμένη ἑβδομάδα]
  since we arrived apo t*o*te poo *ftha*ssame [ἀπό
  τότε πού φθάσαμε]
  (because) epee*thee* [ἐπειδή]
sincere eeleekreen*ees* [εἰλικρινής]
  yours sincerely eeleekreen*a* theek*os* sas
  [εἰλικρινά δικός σας]
sing tragoot*ho* [τραγουδῶ]
single m*o*nos [μόνος]
  single room mon*o* thoma*tee*o [μονό δωμάτιο]

I'm single *ee*me ele*fth*eros [εἶμαι ἐλεύθερος]
a single to Crete ena ap*l*o ya teen K*ree*tee [ἕνα
ἁπλό γιά τήν Κρήτη]
sink: it sank voo*lee*axe [βούλιαξε]
sir k*ee*ree-e [κύριε]
sister: my sister ee athel*fee* moo [ἡ ἀδελφή μου]
sit: can I sit here? bo*ro* na ka*t*sso et*ho* [μπορῶ
νά κάτσω ἐδῶ]
size me*geth*os [μέγεθος]
skid gleestro [γλυστρῶ]
skin the*rma* [δέρμα]
 skin-diving eepov*ree*kheea ka*ta*theessee
 [ὑποβρύχια κατάδυση]
» *TRAVEL TIP: use of an aqualung requires a permit
 from the police*
skirt ee foosta [ἡ φούστα]
sky o oora*nos* [ὁ οὐρανός]
sleep: I can't sleep the*n* bo*ro* na keem*eetho*
 [δέν μπορῶ νά κοιμηθῶ]
 sleeper *(rail)* vagon lee [βαγκόν λή]
 sleeping bag 'sleeping bag' [σλίπινγκ μπάγκ]
 sleeping pill eepnot*ee*ko kha*pee* [ὑπνοτικό
 χάπι]
 YOU MAY HEAR...
 keem*ee*theekes kala? *did you have a good sleep?*
sleeve to man*ee*kee [τό μανίκι]
slide *(phot)* to 'slide' [τό σλάϊντ]
slow ar*ga* [ἀργά]; **could you speak a little
 slower?** bor*ee*te na mee*la*te pe*eo* ar*ga*?
 [μπορεῖτε νά μηλάτε πιό ἀργά;]
small m*ee*kro [μικρό]
 small change psee*la* [ψιλά]
smell: there's a funny smell meer*ee*zee
 per*ee*-erga [μυρίζει περίεργα]
 it smells vroma*ee* [βρωμάει]
smile *(verb)* khamo*gelo* [χαμογελῶ]
smoke *(noun)* to kap* nee*zma [τό κάπνισμα]
 do you smoke? kapn*ee*zete? [καπνίζετε;]
 can I smoke? bo*ro* na kapn*ee*sso? [μπορῶ νά
 καπνίσω;]

smooth apaloε [ἀπαλός]
snack: can we just have a snack? boroome na
tsseebeessome katee? [μπορούμε νά τσιμπήσομε
κάτι;]
snorkel enas anapnefsteeras [ἕνας
ἀναπνευστήρας]
snow kheeonee [χιόνι]
so: it's so hot today kanee tosse zesstee
seemera [κάνει τόση ζέστη σήμερα]
   not so much okhee tosso polee [ὄχι τόσο πολύ]
   so-so etssee ke etssee [ἔτσι καί ἔτσι]
soap ena sapoonee [ἕνα σαπούνι]
   soap powder aporeepandeeko
   [ἀπορυπαντικό]
sober ksemetheestos [ξεμέθυστος]
sock meea kaltssa [μιά κάλτσα]
soda (water) sotha [σόδα]
soft drink ena mee alko-oleeko poto [ἕνα μή
ἀλκοολικό ποτό]
sole *(of shoe)* sola [σόλα]
   (fish) glossa [γλῶσσα]
   could you put new soles on these? boreete
   na moo valete kenoorgee-es soles safta?
   [μπορεῖτε νά βάλετε καινούργιες σόλες σ' αὐτά;]
some: some people mereekee anthropee
   [μερικοί ἄνθρωποι]
   can I have some? boro na ekho leega? [μπορῶ
   νά ἔχω λίγα;]
   can I have some grapes/some bread? boro
   na ekho leega stafeeleea/leego psomee? [μπορῶ
   νά ἔχω λίγα σταφύλια/λίγο ψωμί;]
   can I have some more? boro na ekho leego
   akomee? [μπορῶ νά ἔχω λίγο ἀκόμη;]
   that's some drink! afto eene poto! [αὐτό εἶναι
   ποτό!]
somebody kapeeos [κάποιος]
something katee [κάτι]
sometime kambossee ora [κάμποση ὥρα]
   sometimes kameea fora [καμιά φορά]
somewhere kapoo [κάπου]

son: my son o yee-*os* moo [ὁ γιός μου]
song to trago*othee* [τό τραγούδι]
soon s*ee*ntoma [σύντομα]
  as soon as possible *o*sso to theenat*o*
  seendom*o*tera [ὅσο τό δυνατό συντομώτερα]
  sooner pee*o* nor*ee*s [πιό νωρίς]
sore: it's sore pon*a*ee [πονάει]
  sore throat pon*o*lemos [πονόλεμος]
sorry: (I'm) sorry leep*a*me [λυπάμαι]
sort: this sort af*to* to *ee*thos [αὐτό τό εἶδος]
  what sort of . . .? tee *ee*thos . . .? [τί
  εἶδος . . .;]
  will you sort it out? *th*a to kanon*ee*ssees? [θά
  τό κανονίσεις;]
soup s*oo*pa [σούπα]
sour ks*ee*n*o* [ξυνό]
south o n*o*tos [ὁ νότος]
South Africa Not*ee*os Afr*ee*kee [Νότιος
  'Αφρική]
South African Not*ee*oAfreekanos
  [ΝοτιοΑφρικανός]
souvenir *e*na en*thee*meeo [ἕνα ἐνθύμιο]
spade *e*na ftee*a*ree [ἕνα φτιάρι]
spanner *e*na kleeth*ee* [ἕνα κλειδί]
spare: spare part andalakteek*o*
  [ἀνταλλακτικό]
  spare wheel ee rez*e*rva [ἡ ρεζέρβα]
spark(ing) plug to boozee [τό μπουζί]
speak: do you speak English? meel*a*te
  agleek*a*? [μιλάτε 'Αγγλικά;]
  I don't speak . . . then meel*o* . . . [δέν
  μιλῶ . . .]
special eeth*ee*-eteros [ἰδιαίτερος]
specialist eeth*ee*k*os* [εἰδικός]
specially eeth*ee*-eteros [ἰδιαιτέρως]
spectacles ta yee-ale*a* [τά γυαλιά]
speed ee takh*ee*tees [ἡ ταχύτης]
  he was speeding *e*trekhe [ἔτρεχε]
  speed limit *o*reeo takh*ee*teetos [ὅριο
  ταχύτητος]

speedometer to kon*t*er [τό κοντέρ]
see **driving**
spend *(money)* ksoth*e*vo [ξοδεύω]
spice bakhar*ee*ko [μπαχαρικό]
  is it spicy? *e*khee bakhareek*a*? [ἔχει
  μπαχαρικά;]
  it's too spicy *e*khee pol*l*a bakhareek*a* [ἔχει
  πολλά μπαχαρικά]
spider m*ee*a arakhn*ee* [μιά ἀράχνη]
spirits *(drink)* alko-ol*ee*ka pota [ἀλκοολικά
  ποτά]
spoon *e*na koota*lee* [ἔνα κουτάλι]
sprain: I've sprained it to strambo*o*leexa [τό
  στραμπούληξα]
spring ee peeg*ee* [ἡ πηγή]
  (season) a*nee*exee [ἄνοιξη]
square *(in town)* ee plat*ee*a [ἡ πλατεῖα]
  2 square metres th*ee*o tetragoneek*a* m*e*tra
  [δύο τετραγωνικά μέτρα]
stairs ee ska*le*s [οἱ σκάλες]
stale baya*tee*ko [μπαγιάτικο]
stalls plat*ee*a [πλατεῖα]
stamp *e*na grammatos*see*mo [ἔνα
  γραμματόσημο]
  two stamps for England th*ee*o
  grammatos*see*ma ya teen Ang*lee*a [δύο
  γραμματόσημα γιά τήν 'Αγγλία]
standard stan*d*ard [στάνταρ]
star to *a*sstro [τό ἄστρο]
starboard thex*ee*a plev*ra* pl*ee*oo [δεξιά πλευρά
  πλοίου]
start ksek*ee*no [ξεκινῶ]
  my car won't start to aftok*ee*neeto moo then
  ksek*ee*na*ee* [τό αὐτοκίνητό μου δέν ξεκινάει]
  when does it start? p*o*te ark*hee*zee? [πότε
  ἀρχίζει;]
starter ee m*ee*za [ἡ μίζα]
starving: I'm starving peth*e*no tees p*ee*nas
  [πεθαίνω τῆς πείνας]
station o sta*th*mos [ὁ σταθμός]

statue to agalma [τό ἄγαλμα]
stay: we enjoyed our stay theeaskethassame
teen theeamonee mas [διασκεδάσαμε τήν
διαμονή μας]
   stay there meene ekee [μεῖνε ἐκεῖ]
   I'm staying at Hotel... meno sto
   ksenothokheeo . . . [μένω στό ξενοδοχεῖο . . .]
steak meea breezola [μιά μπριζόλα]
   YOU MAY HEAR . . .
   pos tee thelete? *how would you like it done?*
   kala pseemenee? *well done?*
   okhee polee pseemenee? *rare?*
» *TRAVEL TIP: a rare steak will be very rare!*
steep apotomo [ἀπότομο]
steering seesteema thee-eftheensees [τό
σύστημα διεύθυνσης]
   steering wheel to teemonee [τό τιμόνι]
step *(noun)* to skalee [τό σκαλί]
stereo stereofoneeko seengroteema
[στερεοφωνικό συγκρότημα]
sterling ee sterleena [ή στερλίνα]
stewardess ee a-erosseenothos [ή ἀεροσυνοδός]
sticking plaster lefkoplast [λευκοπλάστ]
sticky kolothees [κολλώδης]
stiff alee-yeestos [ἀλύγιστος]
still: keep still stassoo akeeneetos [στάσου
ἀκίνητος]; **I'm still here** eeme akomee etho
[εἶμαι ἀκόμη ἐδῶ]
stink *(noun)* broma [βρῶμα]
stolen: my wallet's been stolen moo klepsane
to portofolee [μοῦ κλέψανε τό πορτοφόλι]
stomach to stomakhee [τό στομάχι]
   I have stomach-ache ponaee to stomakhee
   moo [πονάει τό στομάχι μου]
   **have you got something for an upset
   stomach?** ekhete kanena farmako ya pono
   stomakheeoo? [ἔχετε κανένα φάρμακο γιά πόνο
   στομαχιοῦ;]
stone meea petra [μιά πέτρα]
» *TRAVEL TIP: 1 stone = 6.35 kilos*

stop: stop! stamata [σταμάτα]
  stop-over stamateema [σταμάτημα]
  (overnight) theeaneekterefssee
  [διανυκτέρευση]
  do you stop near . . . ? stamatate konda . . .?
  [σταματάτε κοντά . . .;]
storm ee *thee*-ela [ἡ θύελλα]
straight eesseea [ἴσια]
  go straight on peegenete eesseea [πηγαίνετε
  ἴσια]
  straight away amessos [ἀμέσως]
  straight whisky sketo whisky [σκέτο οὐΐσκυ]
strange paraxenos [παράξενος]
stranger ksenos [ξένος]; **I'm a stranger
  here** eeme ksenos etho [εἶμαι ξένος ἐδῶ]
strawberry ee fraoola [ἡ φράουλα]
street o thromos [ὁ δρόμος]
string: have you got any string? ekhete
  ka*th*oloo spango? [ἔχετε καθόλου σπάγγο;]
stroke: he's had a stroke epa*th*e prosbolee
  [ἔπαθε προσβολή]
strong theenatos [δυνατός]
student feeteetees [φοιτητής]
stung: I've been stung me tsseembeesse [μέ
  τσίμπησε]
stupid vlakas [βλάκας]
such: such a lot tosso pola [τόσο πολλά]
suddenly ksafneeka [ξαφνικά]
sugar ee zakharee [ἡ ζάχαρη]
suit *(man's)* ena koostoomee [ἕνα κουστούμι]
  (woman's) to tayer [τό ταγιέρ]
  suitcase ee valeedza [ἡ βαλίτσα]
suitable kataleelos [κατάλληλος]
summer to kalokeree [τό καλοκαίρι]
sun o eeleeos [ὁ ἥλιος]
  in the sun ston eeleeo [στόν ἥλιο]
  out of the sun steen skeea [στή σκιά]
  sunbathe eeleea*th*erapeea [ἡλιοθεραπεία]
  sunburn kamenos apo ton eeleeo [καμμένος
  ἀπό τόν ἥλιο]

sunglasses ya-lee*a* eel*ee*oo [γιαλιά ἥλίου]
sunstroke eel*ee*assee [ἡλίαση]
suntan oil l*a*thee eel*ee*oo [λάδι ἡλίου]
Sunday Keereeak*ee* [Κυριακή]
supermarket to supermarket [τό σούπερ
μάρκετ]
supper to th*ee*pno [τό δεῖπνο]
sure: I'm not sure then *ee*me v*e*veos [δέν εἶμαι
βέβαιος]; **sure!** v*e*veos! [βεβαίως!]
are you sure? *ee*sse v*e*veos? [εἶσαι βέβαιος;]
surfboard to kano [τό κανό]
surfing: to go surfing p*a*o serf*ee*ng [πάω
σέρφινγκ]
surname ep*ee*th*e*to [ἐπίθετο]
swearword mee*a* vreess*ee*a [μιά βρισιά]
sweat *(verb)* eethr*o*no [ἱδρώνω]
sweet: it's too sweet *ee*ne pol*ee* gleeko [εἶναι
πολύ γλυκό]
(dessert) ep*ee*th*o*rpeeo [ἐπιδόρπιο]
sweets karam*e*les [καραμέλες]
swerve: I had to swerve epr*e*pe na parekl*ee*no
[ἔπρεπε νά παρεκλίνω]
swim: I'm going for a swim p*a*o ya kol*ee*mbee
[πάω γιά κολύμπι]
let's go for a swim ,p*a*me ya kol*ee*mbee [πάμε
γιά κολύμπι]
swimming costume to ma-ye-*o* [τό μαγιό]
switch o theeak*o*ptees [ὁ διακόπτης]
to switch on/off an*a*vo/sv*ee*no [ἀνάβω/σβήνω]
table to trap*e*zee [τό τραπέζι]
a table for 4 *e*na trap*e*zee ya t*e*sserees [ἕνα
τραπέζι γιά τέσσερις]
table wine epeetrap*e*zeeo krass*ee*
[ἐπιτραπέζιο κρασί]
take p*e*rno [παίρνω]
can I take this with me? boro na p*a*ro aft*o*
maz*ee* moo? [μπορῶ νά πάρω αὐτό μαζί μου;]
will you take me to the airport? bor*ee*te na
me p*a*rete sto a-erothr*o*meeo? [μπορεῖτε νά μέ
πάρετε στό ἀεροδρόμειο;]

how long will it take? posseen ora tha paree?
[πόσην ὥρα θά πάρει;]
somebody has taken my bags kapeeos peere
tees valeedzes moo [κάποιος πῆρε τίς βαλίτσες
μου]
can I take you out tonight? boro na se paro
exo seemera to vrathee? [μπορῶ νά σέ πάρω ἔξω
σήμερα τό βράδι;]
talcum powder poothra talk [πούδρα τάλκ]
talk *(verb)* meelo [μιλῶ]
tall pseelos [ψηλός]
tampons tampon [ταμπόν]
tan mavreesma apo ton eeleeo [μαύρισμα ἀπό τόν
ἥλιο]
I want to get a tan thelo na mavreesso [θέλω
νά μαυρίσω]
tank *(of car)* to depozeeto [τό ντεπόζιτο]
tap ee vreessee [ἡ βρίση]
tape ee teneea [ἡ ταινία]
tape-recorder to magneetofono [τό
μαγνητόφωνο]
tariff tareefa [ταρίφα]
taste *(noun)* ye-fssee [γεύση]
can I taste it? boro na to thokeemasso? [μπορῶ
νά τό δοκιμάσω;]
it tastes horrible/very nice ekhee apesseea
ye-fssee/polee orea [ἔχει ἀπαίσια γεύση/πολύ
ὡραία]
taxi ena taxee [ἕνα ταξί]
will you get me a taxi? tha moo kalessete ena
taxee? [θά μου καλέσετε ἕνα ταξί;]
where can I get a taxi? poo boro na vro ena
taxee? [πού μπορῶ νά βρῶ ἕνα ταξί;]
taxi-driver o taxeedzees [ὁ ταξιτζής]
tea tssaee [τσάϊ]
could I have a cup/pot of tea? boro na ekho
ena fleedzanee/meea tsaye-era tssaee? [μπορῶ
νά ἔχω ἕνα φλιτζάνι/μιά τσαγιέρα τσάϊ;]
with milk/lemon me gala/lemone [μέ
γάλα/λεμόνι]

teach: could you teach me? bor*ee*s na me
  theeth*a*xees? [μπορεῖς νά μέ διδάξεις;]
  could you teach me Greek? bor*ee*s na me
  theeth*a*xees elee*nee*k*a*? [μπορεῖς νά μέ διδάξεις
  ῾Ελληνικά;]
teacher o th*a*skalos [ὁ δάσκαλος]
telegram *e*na teelegr*a*feema [ἕνα τηλεγράφημα]
  I want to send a telegram *the*lo na st*ee*lo *e*na
  teelegr*a*feema [θέλω νά στήλω ἕνα
  τηλεγράφημα]
telephone *(noun)* to tee*le*fono [τό τηλέφωνο]
  can I make a phone-call? boro na
  teelefon*ee*sso? [μπορῶ νά τηλεφωνήσω;]
  can I speak to Maria? boro na mee*lee*sso stee
  Maria [μπορῶ νά μιλήσω στή Μαρία]
  could you get the number for me? bor*ee*te
  na moo p*a*rete ton ar*ee*th*mo*? [μπορεῖτε νά μου
  πάρετέ τόν ἀριθμό;]
  telephone directory o teelefon*ee*k*os*
  kat*a*logos [ὁ τηλεφωνικός κατάλογος]
» *TRAVEL TIP: two types of phone; one with the same
  dialling method as in the UK; but if you don't get
  a tone when you lift the receiver then put money
  in before dialling; code for UK is 0044, dropping
  first 0 of UK area code*
television ee tee*lee*orassee [ἡ τηλεόραση]
  I'd like to watch television *thathe*la na th*o*
  tee*lee*orassee [θάθελα νά δῶ τηλεόραση]
tell: could you tell me where . . .? bor*ee*te na
  moo p*ee*te poo . . .? [μπορεῖτε νά μου πῆτε
  ποῦ . . .;]
temperature *(weather etc)* ee th*e*rmokrass*ee*a
  [ἡ θερμοκρασία]
  he's got a temperature *e*khee peer*e*to [ἔχει
  πυρετό]
temple o na*o*s [ὁ ναός]
tennis *te*nnis [τέννις]
  tennis court ye-petho *te*nnis [γήπεδο τέννις]
  tennis racket rak*e*ta *te*nnis [ρακέτα τέννις]
  tennis ball b*a*la too *te*nnis [μπάλλα τοῦ τέννις]

....

tent ee te*nta* [ἡ τέντα]
terminus to te*rma* [τό τέρμα]
terrible fove*ró* [φοβερό]
terrific exereteeko [ἐξεραιτικό]
than ap*o* [ἀπό]
   bigger/older than ... megal*ee*teros/
   megal*ee*teros ap*o* ...
   [μεγαλύτερος/μεγαλύτερος ἀπό . . .]
thanks, thank you efkhare*esto* [εὐχαριστῶ]
   no thank you o*khee* efkhare*esto* [ὄχι . . .]
   thank you very much efkhare*esto* pol*ee*
   [εὐχαριστῶ πολύ]
   thank you for your help efkhare*esto* ya teen
   vo*eethee*a sas [εὐχαριστῶ γιά τήν βοήθειά σας]
   YOU MAY THEN HEAR ...
   parakal*o* *you're welcome*
that eke*eno* [ἐκεῖνο]
   that man/that table eke*e*nos o
   *a*nthras/eke*e*no to trape*zee* [ἐκεῖνος ὁ
   ἄνδρας/ἐκεῖνο τό τραπέζι]
   I would like that one *that*he*la* eke*eno*
   [θἄθελα ἐκεῖνο]
   how do you say that? pos to le*ne* eke*eno*? [πῶς
   τό λέτε ἐκεῖνο;]
   I think that ... nom*ee*zo ot*ee* [νομίζω ὅτι . . .]
the o, ee, to [ὁ, ἡ, τό]; *(plural)* ee, ee, ta
   [οἱ, οἱ, τά]
theatre to *the*atro [τό θέατρο]
their too*s* [τούς]
   it's their bag/it's theirs *ee*ne ee tss*a*nda
   toos/*ee*ne theeke*e*a toos [εἶναι ἡ τσάντα
   τους/εἶναι δικιά τους]
them: I've lost them toos, tees, t*a* ekhass*a*
   [τους, τίς, τά ἔχασα]
   with them maz*ee* toos [μαζί τους]
   who? – them pee-*ee*? aft*ee*, aft*es*, aft*a* [ποιοί;
   αὐτοί, αὐτές, αὐτά]
then to*te* [τότε]
there eke*e* [ἐκεῖ]; **how do I get there?** pos*tha*
   pa*o* eke*e*? [πώς θά πάω ἐκεῖ;]

is there . . ./are there . . .? eep**a**rkhee . . ./
eep**a**rkhoon . . .? [ὑπάρχει . . ./ὑπάρχουν . . .;]
there is . . ./there are . . . eep**a**rkhee . . ./
eep**a**rkhoon . . . [ὑπάρχει . . ./ὑπάρχουν . . .]
there you are *(giving something)* or**ee**ste
[ὁρίστε]
these aft**ee**, aft**e**s, aft**a** [αὐτοί, αὐτές, αὐτά]
these apples aft**a** ta m**ee**la [αὐτά τά μῆλα]
can I take these? boro na p**a**ro aft**a** [μπορῶ νά
π**a**ρω αὐτά]
these people aft**ee** ee **a**nthropee [αὐτοί οἱ
ἄνθρωποι]
these bags aft**e**s ee ts**a**ndes [αὐτές οἱ τσάντες]
they aft**ee**, aft**e**s, aft**a** [αὐτοί, αὐτές, αὐτά]
they are . . . **ee**ne . . . [εἶναι . . .]
thick pakh**ee** [παχύ]
(stupid) khaz**o**s [χαζός]
thief o kleft**ee**s [ὁ κλέφτης]
thigh o me**e**ros [ὁ μηρός]
thin ath**ee**natos [ἀδύνατος]
thing pr**a**gma [πρᾶγμα]
I've lost all my things **e**khassa **o**la moo ta
pr**a**gmata [ἔχασα ὅλα μου τά πράγματα]
think sk**e**ptome [σκέπτομαι]
I'll think it over *th*a to skef-th**o** [θά τό σκεφθῶ]
I think so/I don't think so nom**ee**zo/then
nom**ee**zo [νομίζω/δέν νομίζω]
third *(adjective)* tr**ee**tos [τρίτος]
thirsty theeps**a**zm**e**nos [διψασμένος]
I'm thirsty theeps**o** [διψῶ]
this aft**o**s, aft**ee**, aft**o** [αὐτός, αὐτή, αὐτό]
this hotel/this street aft**o** to
ksenothokh**ee**o/aft**o**s o thr**o**mos [αὐτό τό
ξενοδοχεῖο/αὐτός ὁ δρόμος]
can I have this one? boro na **e**kho aft**o** eth**o**?
[μπορῶ νά ἔχω αὐτό ἐδῶ;]
this is my wife/this is Mr . . . aft**ee** **ee**ne ee
ye-n**e**ka moo/aft**o**s **ee**ne o k**e**ere**e**os . . . [αὐτή
εἶναι ἡ γυναίκα μου/αὐτός εἶναι ὁ Κύριος . . .]
is this . . .? **ee**ne aft**o** . . .? [εἶναι αὐτό . . .;]

those *see* **these**
  no, not these, those! okhee, okhee afta,
  ekeena! [ὄχι, ὄχι αὐτά, ἐκεῖνα!]
thread *(noun)* meea klosstee [μιά κλωστή]
throat o lemos [ὁ λεμός]
throttle *(motorbike, boat)* gazee [γκάζι]
through theea messoo [διά μέσου]
throw *(verb)* reekhno [ρίχνω]
thumb o andeekheeras [ὁ ἀντίχειρας]
thunder *(noun)* ee vrondee [ἡ βροντή]
  thunderstorm kakokereea [κακοκαιρία]
Thursday Pemtee [Πέμπτη]
ticket to eesseeteereeo [τό εἰσιτήριο]
  (cloakroom) o areethmos [ὁ ἀριθμός]
tie *(necktie)* ee gravata [ἡ γραβάτα]
tight *(clothes)* steno [στενό]
tights kaltsson [καλτσόν]
time ora, khronos [ὥρα, χρόνος]
  what's the time? tee ora eene? [τί ὥρα εἶναι;]
  I haven't got time then ekho khrono [δέν ἔχω
  χρόνο]
  for the time being ya teen ora [γιά τήν ὥρα]
  this time/last time/next time aftee tee
  fora/teen perasmenee fora/teen alee fora [αὐτή
  τή φορά/τήν περασμένη φορά/τήν ἄλλη φορά]
  3 times trees fores [τρεῖς φορές]
  have a good time kalee theeaskethassee
  [καλή διασκέδαση]
  timetable to programa [τό πρόγραμμα]
»*TRAVEL TIP: how to tell the time*
  it's one o'clock eene ee ora meea [εἶναι ἡ ὥρα
  μία]
  it's two/three/four/five/six o'clock eene ee
  ora theeo/trees/tesserees/pende/exee [εἶναι ἡ
  ὥρα δύο/τρεῖς/τέσσερις/πέντε/ἔξι]
  it's 5/10/20/25 past seven eene epta ke
  pende/theka/eekossee/eekosse pende [εἶναι ἑπτά
  καί πέντε/δέκα/εἴκοσι/εἴκοσι πέντε]
  it's quarter past eight/eight fifteen eene
  okto ke tetarto/okto ke theka pende [εἶναι ὀκτώ

καί τέταρτο/ὀκτώ καί δέκα πέντε]
it's half past nine/nine thirty eene enea ke
meessee/enea ke treeanda [εἶναι ἐννέα καί
μισή/ἐννέα καί τριάντα]
it's 25/20/10/5 to ten eene theka para eekosse
pende/eekossee/theka/pende [εἶναι δέκα παρά
εἴκοσι πέντε/εἴκοσι/δεκα/πέντε]
it's quarter to eleven/10.45 eene endeka para
tetarto/endeka ke saranda pende [εἶναι ἔντεκα
παρά τέταρτο/ἔντεκα καί σαράντα πέντε]
it's twelve o'clock eene eeora thotheka [εἶναι
ἡ ὥρα δώδεκα]
tin (can) meea konsserva [μιά κονσέρβα]
   tin-opener to aneekteeree [τό ἀνοιχτήρι]
tip (noun) to feelethoreema [τό φιλοδώρημα]
   is the tip included? pereelamvanete to
   feelothoreema? [περιλαμβάνεται τό
   φιλοδώρημα;]
» TRAVEL TIP: tip the same people as in UK
tired koorasmenos [κουρασμένος]
   I'm tired eeme koorasmenos [εἶμαι
   κουρασμένος]
tissues khartomantheela [χαρτομάνδηλα]
to: to Crete/England ye-a teen
   Kreetee/Angleea [γιά τή Κρήτη/Ἀγγλία]
toast tost [τόστ]
tobacco kapnos [καπνός]
tobacconist's to kapnopoleeo [τό καπνοπωλεῖο]
» TRAVEL TIP: buy tobacco from street kiosks called
   'to pereeptero' [τό περίπτερο]; see kiosk
today seemera [σήμερα]
toe to thakteelo too potheeoo [τό δάκτυλο τοῦ
   ποδιοῦ]
together mazee [μαζί]
   we're together eemaste mazee [εἴμαστε μαζί]
   can we pay all together? boroome na
   pleerosome ola mazee? [μπορούμε νά
   πληρώσωμε ὅλα μαζί;]
toilet ee tooaleta [ἡ τουαλέττα]
   where are the toilets? poo ene ee tooaleta?

[πού εἶναι ἡ τουαλέττα;]
I have to go to the toilet prepee na pao stee
tooaleta [πρέπει νά πάω στή τουαλέττα]
there's no toilet paper then eeparkhee
khartee tooaletas [δέν ὑπάρχει χαρτί
τουαλέπας]
» *TRAVEL TIP: see* **public**
tomato domata [ἡ τομάτα]
    tomato ketchup ketchup [κέτσαπ]
    tomato juice domatozoomo [τοματόζουμο]
tomorrow avreeo [αὔριο]
    tomorrow morning/tomorrow afternoon/
    tomorrow evening avreeo to proee/avreeo to
    apoye-vma/avreeo to vrathee [αὔριο τό πρωΐ/
    αὔριο τό ἀπόγευμα/αὔριο τό βράδι]
    the day after tomorrow methavreeo
    [μεθαύριο]
    see you tomorrow tha se thoavreeo [θά σέ δῶ
    αὔριο]
ton enas tonos [ἕνας τόνος]
» *TRAVEL TIP: 1 ton = 1016 kilos*
tongue ee glossa [ἡ γλῶσσα]
tonic (water) tonic [τόνικ]
tonight seemera to vrathee [σήμερα τό βράδυ]
tonne enas tonnos [ἕνας τόννος]
» *TRAVEL TIP: 1 tonne = 1000 kilos = metric ton*
tonsilitis ameegthaleetees [ἀμυγδαλῖτις]
too polee [πολύ]; *(also)* epeessees [ἐπίσης]
    that's too much afto eene para polee [αὐτό
    εἶναι πάρα πολύ]
tool ergaleeo [ἐργαλεῖο]
tooth to thondee [τό δόντι]
    I've got toothache ekho ponothondo [ἔχω
    πονόδοντο]
    toothbrush ee othondovoortssa
    [ἡ ὀδοντόβουρτσα]
    toothpaste ee othondokrema [ἡ ὀδοντόκρεμα]
top: on top of . . . pano apo . . . [πάνω ἀπό . . .]
    on the top floor sto pano patoma [στό πάνω
    πάτωμα]

at the top stee korfee [στή κορφή]
total *(noun)* to seenolo [τό σύνολο]
tough *(meat)* skleero [σκληρό]
tour *(noun)* ee pereeotheea [ή περιοδία]
  we'd like to go on a tour of the island
  *the*lome na pame pereeotheea sto neessee
  [θέλομε νά πάμε περιοδία στό νησί]
  we're touring around pereeothevome
  [περιοδεύομε]
tourist o tooreestas [ό τουρίστας]
  I'm a tourist eeme tooreestas [εἶμαι τουρίστας]
  tourist office grafeeo tooreesmoo [γραφεῖο
  τουρισμοῦ]
tow *(verb)* reemoolko [ρυμουλκῶ]
  can you give me a tow? borees na me
  reemoolkeessees? [μπορεῖς νά μέ ρυμουλκήσεις;]
  towrope skheenee reemoolkeesseos [σχοινί
  ρυμουλκήσεως]
towards pros [πρός]
  he was coming straight towards me
  erkhondan kat' eftheean pros ta pano moo
  [ἐρχόνταν κατ' εὐθεῖαν πρός τά πάνω μου]
towel ee petsseta [ή πετσέτα]
town ee polee [ή πόλη]
  in town stee polee [στή πόλη]
  would you take me into the town? boreete
  na me parete stee polee? [μπορεῖτε νά μέ πάρετε
  στή πόλη;]
traditional patroparathotos [πατροπαράδοτος]
  a traditional Greek meal ena patroparathoto
  Eleeneeko fageeto [ἕνα πατροπαράδοτο
  Ἑλληνικό φαγητό]
traffic ee keekloforeea [ή κυκλοφορία]
  traffic lights fanareea trokheas [φανάρια
  τροχαίας]
train to treno [τό τραῖνο]
tranquillizers katapraeendeeka
  [καταπραϋντικά]
translate metefrazo [μεταφράζω]
  would you translate that for me? boreete na

moo metafrassete aft♢? [μπορεῖτε νά μου
μεταφράσετε αὐτό;]
transmission *(of car)* ee takheeteetes [οἱ
ταχύτητες]
travel agent's praktoreeo taxeetheeon
[πρακτορεῖο ταξιδίων]
traveller's cheque taxeetheeoteekee epeetagee
[ταξιδιωτική ἐπιταγή]
tree to thenthro [τό δένδρο]
tremendous thavmasseea [θαυμάσια]
trim: just a trim, please fresskareesma mono,
parakalo [φρεσκάρισμα μόνο, παρακαλῶ]
trip *(noun)* to taxeethee [τό ταξίδι]
we want to go on a trip to Hydra thelome na
pame ena taxeethee steen Eethra [θέλομε νά
πάμε ἕνα ταξίδι στήν ῞Υδρα]
trouble *(noun)* enokhleessee [ἐνόχληση]
**I'm having trouble with . . . (the
steering/my back)** ekho provleemata
me . . . (to teemonee/teen platee moo) [ἔχω
προβλήματα μέ . . . (τό τιμόνι/τήν πλάτη μου)]
trousers to pantalonee [τό πανταλόνι]
true aleetheeno [ἀληθινό]
it's not true then eene aleetheea [δέν εἶναι
ἀλήθεια]
trunks *(swimming)* to mayee-o [τό μαγιό]
try *(verb)* thokeemazo [δοκιμάζω]
please try parakalo thokeemaste [παρακαλῶ
δοκιμάστε]
can I try it on? boro na to thokeemasso pano
moo? [μπορῶ νά τό δωκιμάσω πάνω μου;]
T-shirt to bloozakee [τό μπλουζάκι]
Tuesday Treetee [Τρίτη]
turn: where do we turn off? poo tha
streepsome? [πού θά στρίψομε;]
he turned without indicating estreepse
khorees na valee seema [ἔστριψε χωρίς νά βάλει
σῆμα]
twice theeo fores [δυό φορές]
twice as much ta theepla [τά διπλά]

twin beds th*ee*o krevat*ee*a [δύο κρεβάτια]
typewriter ee grafomeekhan*ee* [ή γραφομηχανή]
typical teepeek*o* [τυπικό]
tyre l*a*ssteekho [λάστιχο]
   I need a new tyre khree*a*zome ken*oo*ryee-o
   l*a*steekho [χρηάζομε καινούργιο λάστιχο]
» *TRAVEL TIP: tyre pressures*

lb/sq in	18	20	22	24	26	28	30
kg/sq cm	13	1.4	15	1.7	1.8	2	2.1

ugly *a*skheemos [ἄσχημος]
ulcer *e*lkos [ἔλκος]
Ulster Voreeos Irlanth*ee*a [Βόρειος Ἰρλανδία]
umbrella me*a* ombr*e*la [μιά ὀμπρέλλα]
uncle: my uncle o th*ee*os moo [ὁ θείος μου]
uncomfortable *a*volos [ἄβολος]
unconscious an*e*ssth*ee*tos [ἀναίσθητος]
under ap*o* kato [ἀπό κάτω]
underdone meessopseem*e*no [μισοψημένο]
underground *(rail)* o eepogeeos [ὁ ὑπόγειος]
understand: I understand katalav*e*no
   [καταλαβαίνω]
   I don't understand then katalav*e*no [δέν
   καταλαβαίνω]
   do you understand? katalav*e*nees?
   [καταλαβαίνεις;]
undo l*e*eno [λύνω]
unfriendly mee feeleek*o*s [μή φιλικός]
unhappy theesteekheesm*e*nos [δυστυχισμένος]
United States Inomenes Pol*e*etee-es
   [Ἡνωμένες Πολιτείες]
unleaded am*o*leevtho petr*e*leo [ἀνόλυβδο
   πετρέλαιο]
unlock ksekleeth*o*no [ξεκλειδώνω]
until m*e*khree [μέχρι]
unusual asseen*ee*th*ee*stos [ἀσυνήθιστος]
up p*a*no [πάνω]
   he's not up yet then ks*ee*pneesse ak*o*mee [δέν
   ξύπνησε ἀκόμη]
   what's up? tee g*ee*netee? [τί γίνεται;]
upside-down ta p*a*no kato [τά πάνω κάτω]

upstairs p*a*no [πάνω]
urgent ep*ee*gon [ἐπείγων]
us mas [μας]
use: can I u**se . . .?** b*o*ro na khr*ee*ssemop*ee*-
   *ee*sso . . .? [μπορῶ νά χρησιμοποιήσω . . .;]
useful khr*ee*sseemos [χρήσιμος]
usual seen*ee*th*ee*smeno [συνηθισμένο]
   as usual *o*pos seen*ee*th*o*s [ὅπως συνήθως]
usually seen*ee*th*o*s [συνήθως]
U-turn strof*ee* ep*ee* t*o*poo [στροφή ἐπί τόπου]
vacancy ken*ee* th*e*ssee [κενή θέση]
   do you have any vacancies? *e*khete ken*e*s
   th*e*ssees? [ἔχετε κενές θέσεις;]
vacate *(room)* athe*a*zo [ἀδειάζω]
vaccination envol*ee*asmos [ἐμβολιασμός]
vacuum flask to th*e*rmos [τό θέρμος]
valid eng*ee*ros [ἔγκυρος]
   how long is it valid for? ya p*o*sso eeskh*ee*-ee?
   [γιά πόσο ἰσχύει;]
valuable pol*ee*teemos [πολύτιμος]
   will you look after my valuables? th*a*
   pros*e*ksete ta teemalf*ee* moo? [θά προσέξετε τά
   τιμαλφῆ μου;]
value ee ax*ee*a [ἡ ἀξία]
valve ee valv*ee*tha [ἡ βαλβίδα]
van to trokh*o*speeto [τό τροχόσπιτο]
   (delivery) to fort*ee*go [τό φορτηγό]
vanilla van*ee*leea [βανίλια]
varicose veins flev*ee*tees [φλεβίτης]
veal veeth*e*lo [βιδέλο]
vegetables lakhan*ee*ka [λαχανικά]
vegetarian khortof*a*gos [χορτοφάγος]
ventilator o anem*ee*steeras [ὁ ἀνεμιστήρας]
very pol*ee* [πολύ]
   very much p*a*ra pol*ee* [πάρα πολύ]
via the*a* m*e*ssoo [διά μέσου]
village to khor*ee*o [τό χωριό]
vine ee kleematar*ee*a [ἡ κληματαριά]
vinegar to ks*ee*thee [τό ξύδι]
vineyard to amb*e*lee [τό ἀμπέλι]

vintage o treegos [ὁ τρύγος]
violent vee-eos [βίαιος]
visibility oratotees [ὁρατότης]
visit *(verb)* epeeskeptome [ἐπισκέπτομαι]
vodka votka [βότκα]
voice fonee [φωνή]
voltage volt [βόλτ]
waist messee [μέση]
» *TRAVEL TIP: waist measurements*

UK	24	26	28	30	32	34	36	38
Greece	61	66	71	76	80	87	91	97

wait: will we have to wait long? *th*a prepee na
    pereemenoome polee? [θά πρέπει νά
    περιμένουμε πολύ;]
    wait for me pereemene me [περίμενέ με]
    I'm waiting for a friend/my wife pereemeno
    ena feelo/tee yeeneka moo [περιμένω ἕνα
    φίλο/τή γυναίκα μου]
waiter o serveetoros [ὁ σερβιτόρος]
    waiter! garson! [γκαρσόν!]
» *TRAVEL TIP: it is no longer acceptable (as some
    books say) to clap your hands for the waiter*
waitress serveetora [σερβιτόρα]
    waitress! thespeenees! [δεσποινίς]
wake: will you wake me up at 7.30? boreete na
    me kseepneessete stees epta ke meessee?
    [μπορεῖτε νά μέ ξυπνήσετε στίς 7 καί μισή;]
Wales Ooaleea [Οὐαλλία]
walk: can we walk there? boroome na pame
    perpatontas ekee? [μπορούμε νά πάμε
    περπατώντας ἐκεῖ;]
    are there any good walks around here?
    eeparkhoon ore-es voltes etho yee-ro?
    [ὑπάρχουν ὡραῖες βόλτες ἐδῶ γύρω;]
    walking shoes papootsseea pereepatoo
    [παπούτσια περιπάτου]
    walking stick to bastoonee [τό μπαστούνι]
wall o teekhos [ὁ τοῖχος]
wallet to portofolee [τό πορτοφόλι]
want: I want a... theloena... [θέλω ἕνα...]

I want to talk to the consul *the*lo na
meel*ee*sso ston pr*o*xeno [θέλω νά μιλήσω στόν
πρόξενο]
   what do you want? tee *the*lees? [τί θέλεις;]
I don't want to then *the*lo na [δέν θέλω νά]
he wants to ... *the*lee na ... [θέλει νά . . .]

warm khl*ee*aros [χλιαρός]

warning proeethop*ee*-eessee [προειδοποίηση]

was: I was/he was/it was *ee*moon/*ee*ssoon/
*ee*tan [ἤμουν/ἤσουν/ἤταν]

wash: can you wash these for me? bor*ee*te na
moo pl*ee*nete afta? [μπορεῖτε νά μοῦ πλύνετε
αὐτά;]
   where can I wash? poo boro na plee*tho*? [ποῦ
μπορῶ νά πλυθῶ;]
washing powder aporeepand*ee*ko
[ἀπορυπαντικό]

washer *(for nut)* ee roth*e*la [ἡ ροδέλλα]

wasp ee sf*ee*ka [ἡ σφῆκα]

watch *(wrist-)* to rol*o*ee [τό ρολόϊ]
   will you watch my bags for me? *tha*
bor*oo*ssate na moo pros*e*khete tees ts*a*ndes? [θά
μπορούσατε νά μοῦ προσέξετε τίς τσάντες;]
watch out! pross*e*khe![πρόσεχε!]

water to n*e*ro [τό νερό]
   can I have some water? boro n*a*kho l*ee*go
nero? [μπορῶ νἄχω λίγο νερό;]
hot and cold running water zesto ke kr*ee*o
trekh*oo*meno nero [ζεστό καί κρύο τρεχούμενο
νερό]
waterproof athee*a*vrokho [ἀδιάβροχο]
waterskiing *tha*lasseeo skee [θαλάσσιο σκύ]

way: we'd like to eat the Greek way *the*lo na
f*a*o Eleen*ee*ko fay*e*to [θέλω νά φάω Ἑλληνικό
φαγητό]
   could you tell me the way to ...? bor*ee*te na
moo p*ee*te to thromo ya ...? [μπορεῖτε νά μου
πῆτε τό δρόμο γιά . . .;]
for answers see **where**

we em*ee*s [ἐμεῖς]; **we are** *ee*maste [εἴμαστε]

weak ath*ee*natos [ἀδύνατος]
weather o ker*o*s [ο καιρός]
  what filthy weather! tee ap*e*sseeos ker*o*s
  [τί ἀπαίσιος καιρός]
  what's the weather forecast? tee l*e*-ee to
  meteoroloyeek*o* thelt*ee*o? [τί λέει τό
  μετεωρολογικό δελτεῖο;]
  YOU MAY THEN HEAR . . .
  *th*a kanee z*e*stee *it's going to be hot*
  *th*a vr*e*ksee *it's going to rain*
Wednesday Tetartee [Τετάρτη]
week mee*a* evthom*a*tha [μιά ἑβδομάδα]
  a week today/tomorrow se mee*a*
  evthom*a*tha apo s*ee*mera/a*v*reeo [σέ μιά
  ἑβδομάδα ἀπό σήμερα/αὔριο]
  at the weekend to Savatok*ee*reeako [τό
  Σαββατοκύριακο]
weight to b*a*ros [τό βάρος]
well: I'm not feeling well th*e*n esth*a*nome kal*a*
  [δέν αἰσθάνομαι καλά]
  he's not well th*e*n *ee*ne kal*a* [δέν εἶναι καλά]
  how are you? very well, thanks tee ka*nees*?
  pol*ee* kal*a* efkhareesto [τί κάνεις; πολύ καλά
  εὐχαριστῶ]
  you speak English very well meel*a*te
  Angleek*a* pol*ee* kal*a* [μιλάτε ᾿Αγγλικά πολύ
  καλά]
wellingtons ee galotses [οἱ γαλότσες]
Welsh Ooal*o*s [Οὐαλλός]
were: you were *ee*ssoon [ἤσουν]
  we were *ee*maste [ἤμαστε]
  you were *(plural, polite form)* *ee*ssaste
  [ἤσαστε] **they were** *ee*tan [ἤταν]
west theeteek*a* [δυτικά]
West Indies Theeteekes Inthee-es [Δυτικές
  ᾿Ινδίες]
wet eegr*o*s [ὑγρός]
  we*t* suit mee*a* f*o*rma katath*ee*seos [μία φόρμα
  καταδύσεως]
what tee [τί]

what is that? tee *eene* ek*ee*no? [τί εἶναι ἐκεῖνο;]
what for? ya pe*eo* logo? [γιά ποιό λόγο;]
wheel ee rotha [ἡ ρόδα]
when pote [πότε]
   when is breakfast? pote *eene* to proyevma?
   [πότε εἶναι τό πρόγευμα;]
   when we arrived *o*tan *fth*assame [ὅταν
   φθάσαμε]
where poo [ποῦ]
   where is the post office? poo *eene* to
   takhee*th*rom*eeo*? [ποῦ εἶναι τό ταχυδρομεῖο;]
   YOU MAY THEN HEAR...
   *ee*seea *straight on*
   o th*e*fteros thromos areeestera *the second left*
   o protos thromos thex*ee*a *first right*
   se th*ee*o kheelee*o*metra *two kilometres further*
which pe*eo*s [ποιός]
   which one? pe*eo* ap' ola? [ποιό ἀπ' ὅλα;]
   YOU MAY THEN HEAR...
   aft*o* *this one* ek*ee*no *that one*
whisky whisky [οὐϊσκι]
white *a*spro [ἄσπρο]
who pe*eo*s [ποιός]
   YOU MAY THEN HEAR...
   aft*o*s *him* aft*ee* *her*
whose peean*oo* [ποιανοῦ]
   whose is this? peean*oo* *ee*ne aft*o*? [ποιανοῦ
   εἶναι αὐτό;]
   YOU MAY THEN HEAR...
   *ee*ne too Yan*ee* *it's John's*
   *ee*ne theek*o* moo *it's mine*
why? yat*ee*? [γιατί;]
   why not? yat*ee* *o*khee? [γιατί ὅχι;]
wide plat*ee* [πλατύ]
wife: my wife ee seezeegos moo [ἡ σύζυγός μου]
will: when will it be finished? pote *th*a
   tele*eo*ssee? [πότε θά τελειώσει;]
   will you do it? bor*ee*te na to ka*ne*te? [μπορεῖτε
   νά τό κάνετε;]; **I will come back** *th*a
   epeestr*e*pso [θά ἐπιστρέψω]

wind o *a*nemos [ὁ ἄνεμος]
window to para*th*eero [τό παράθυρο]
  near the window konta sto para*th*eero [κοντά στό παράθυρο]
windscreen to bar-preez [τό μπάρ-πρίζ]
  windscreen wipers ee eealoka*th*areeste*e*res [οἱ ὑαλοκαθαρ_ιστῆρες]
windy feessaee pol*ee* [φυσάει πολύ]
wine to krass*ee* [τό κρασί]
  can I see the wine list? boro na tho ton katalogo ton kraseeon? [μπορῶ νά δῶ τόν κατάλογο τῶν κρασιῶν;]
» *TRAVEL TIP: some well-known types of Greek wine are:*
  *a*spro krass*ee* [ἄσπρο κρασί] *white, dry or sweet*
  kokkino krass*ee* [κόκκινο κρασί] *red, dry or sweet*
  retse*e*na [ρετσίνα] *resinated white wine, very strong and distinctive taste*
  ma*v*rotha*f*nee [μαυροδάφνη] *red dessert wine, very sweet*
  kokeen*e*lee [κοκκινέλι] *red wine sold on draught in ½ litre tin measures*
  bro*o*sko [μπροῦσκο] *red, very dry*
winter o kheem*o*nas [ὁ χειμώνας]
wire *e*na kalo*th*ee*o* [ἔνα καλώδιο]
wish: best wishes pol*e*s ef*kh*es [πολλές εὐχές]
with ma*z*ee [μαζί]
without khor*ee*s [χωρίς]
witness ma*r*teeras [μάρτυρας]
  will you act as a witness for me? bor*e*es na *e*ese marteera*s* moo? [μπορεῖς νά εἶσαι μαρτυράς μου;]
woman ee yeen*e*ka [ἡ γυναῖκα]
  women ee yeen*e*kes [οἱ γυναῖκες]
wonderful *th*avmasseeos [θαυμάσιος]
won't: it won't start then ksekeena*e*e [δέν ξεκινάει]
wood to ks*e*elo [τό ξύλο]; *(trees)* tha*s*os [δάσος]
wool mal*e*e [μαλλί]

word ee leksee [ἡ λέξη]
  I don't know that word then ksero aftee tee
  leksee [δέν ξέρω αὐτή τή λέξη]
work ergazome [ἐργάζομαι]
  it's not working then ergazete [δέν ἐργάζεται]
  I work in London ergazome sto lontheeno
  [ἐργάζομαι στό Λονδίνο]
worry stenokhoreea [στενοχώρια]
  I'm worried about him stenokhoree-eme
  yafton [στενοχωριέμαι γιαὐτόν]
  don't worry meen aneesseekhees [μήν
  ἀνησυχεῖς]
worry beads to komboloee [τό κομπολόϊ]
worse: it's worse eene kheerotera [εἶναι
  χειρότερα]
  he's getting worse kheeroterevee
  [χειροτερεύει]
worst kheeroteros [χειρότερος]
worth: it's not worth that much then akseezee
  tosso polee [δέν ἀξίζει τόσο πολύ]
  is it worthwhile going? akseezee ton kopo na
  pame? [ἀξίζει τόν κόπο νά πάμε;]
wrap: could you wrap it up? boreete na to
  teeleeksete? [μπορεῖτε νά τό τυλίξετε;]
wrench ena kleethe [ἕνα κλειδί]
wrist o karpos [ὁ καρπός]
write grafo [γράφω]
  could you write it down? boreete na moo to
  grapsete? [μπορεῖτε νά μοῦ τό γράψετε;]
  I'll write to you tha soo grapso [θά σοῦ γράψω]
  writing paper epeestolokharto
  [ἐπιστολόχαρτο]
wrong lathos [λάθος]
  I think the bill's wrong nomeezo otee o
  logareeazmos eene lathos [νομίζω ὅτι ὁ
  λογαριασμός εἶναι λάθος]
  there's something wrong with ... egeene
  kapeeo lathos me ... [ἔγινε κάποιο λάθος
  μέ . . .]
  you're wrong kanees lathos [κάνεις λάθος]

sorry, wrong number seegnomee lath os
aree*th*mos [συγγνώμη, λάθος ἀριθμός]
X-ray ee akteenografeea [ἡ ἀκτινογραφία]
yacht to yot [τό γιώτ]
yard ee avlee [ἡ αὐλή]
» *TRAVEL TIP: 1 yard = 91.44 cms = 0.91 m*
year o khronos [ὁ χρόνος]
this year/next year fetos/too khronoo
[φέτος/τοῦ χρόνου]
yellow keetreeno [κίτρινο]
yes ne [ναί]
yesterday kh*thes* [χθές]
the day before yesterday prokh*thes*
[προχθές]
yesterday morning/afternoon kh*thes* to
pro*ee*/to apoyevma [χθές τό πρωΐ/τό ἀπόγευμα]
yet: is it ready yet? ee*nee*teemo? [εἶναι ἕτοιμο;]
not yet okhee akomee [ὄχι ἀκόμη]
yoghurt to yaoortee [τό γιαούρτι]
you ess*ee* [ἐσύ]
(plural, polite form) ess*ees* [ἐσεῖς]
I like you mar*ee*ssees [μ' ἀρέσεις]
with you mazee soo [μαζί σου]
» *TRAVEL TIP: the polite form is used in more
formal situations*
young neos [νέος]
your theeko soo [δικό σου]
(plural, polite form) theeko sas [δικό σας]
is this your camera?, is this yours? aft*ee* ee
fotografeek*ee* meekhan*ee* ee*ne* theek*ee* soo,*ee*ne
theeko soo? [αὐτή ἡ φωτογραφική μηχανή εἶναι
δική σου, εἶναι δικό σου;]
youth hostel ksenonas neon [ξενώνας νέων]
Yugoslavia Yungoslavee a [Γιουγκοσλαβία]
Yugoslavian Yungosla vos [Γιουγκοσλάβος]
zero meethen [μηδέν]
below zero eepo to meethen [ὑπό τό μηδέν]
zip fermooar [φερμουάρ]

GREEK SIGNS AND NOTICES

ΑΙΘΟΥΣΑ ΑΝΑΜΟΝΗΣ *waiting room*
ΑΝΑΧΩΡΗΣΕΙΣ *departures*
ΑΝΟΙΚΤΟΝ *open*
ΑΠΑΓΟΡΕΥΕΤΑΙ Η ΕΙΣΟΔΟΣ *no entry*
ΑΠΑΓΟΡΕΥΕΤΑΙ Η ΚΟΛΥΜΒΗΣΗ *no
  swimming*
ΑΠΑΓΟΡΕΥΟΝΤΑΙ ΟΙ ΚΑΤΑΔΥΣΕΙΣ *no
  diving*
ΑΠΑΓΟΡΕΥΕΤΑΙ ΤΟ ΚΑΠΝΙΣΜΑ *no smoking*
ΑΠΑΓΟΡΕΥΕΤΑΙ Η ΛΗΨΗ
  ΦΩΤΟΓΡΑΦΙΩΝ *no photographs*
ΑΣΤΥΝΟΜΙΑ *police*
ΑΦΙΞΕΙΣ *arrivals*
ΔΙΟΔΙΑ *toll*
ΕΘΝΙΚΗ ΟΔΟΣ *motorway*
ΕΙΣΟΔΟΣ *entrance*
ΕΛΕΥΘΕΡΟΝ *vacant*
ΕΝΟΙΚΙΑΖΟΝΤΑΙ ΔΩΜΑΤΙΑ *rooms to let*
ΕΞΟΔΟΣ *exit*
ΕΞΟΔΟΣ ΚΙΝΔΥΝΟΥ *emergency exit*
ΕΙΣΙΤΗΡΙΑ *tickets*
ΖΕΣΤΟ *hot*
ΚΑΤΕΙΛΗΜΜΕΝΟ *engaged*
ΚΙΝΔΥΝΟΣ *danger*
ΚΛΕΙΣΤΟΝ *closed*
ΚΡΥΟ *cold*
ΜΗ ΕΓΓΙΖΕΤΕ *don't touch*
ΝΟΣΟΚΟΜΕΙΟ *hospital*
ΠΛΗΡΟΦΟΡΙΕΣ *information*
ΠΟΣΙΜΟ ΝΕΡΟ *drinking water*
ΠΡΟΣΟΧΗ *caution*
ΠΡΟΣΟΧΗ ΝΑΡΚΕΣ *caution mines*
ΡΕΣΕΨΙΟΝ *reception*
ΣΥΡΑΤΕ *pull*
ΤΑΜΕΙΟ *cash desk*
ΤΕΛΩΝΕΙΟ *customs*
ΤΟΥΑΛΕΤΕΣ *toilets*
ΩΘΗΣΑΤΕ *push*

0 meethen [μηδέν]
1 ena [ἕνα]
2 theeo [δύο]
3 treea [τρία]
4 tessera [τέσσερα]
5 pende [πέντε]
6 exee [ἕξι]
7 epta [ἑπτά]
8 okto [ὀκτώ]
9 enea [ἐννέα]
10 theka [δέκα]
11 endeka [ἕντεκα]
12 thotheka [δώδεκα]
13 thekatreea [δεκατρία]
14 thekatessera [δεκατέσσερα]
15 thekapende [δεκαπέντε]
16 theaexee [δεκαέξι]
17 thekaepta [δεκαεπτά]
18 thekaokto [δεκαοκτώ]
19 thekaenea [δεκαεννέα]
20 eekossee [εἴκοσι]
21 eekossee ena [εἴκοσι ἕνα]
22 eekossee theeo [εἴκοσι δύο]
23 eekossee treea [εἴκοσι τρία]
24 eekossee tessera [εἴκοσι τέσσερα]
25 eekossee pende [εἴκοσι πέντε]
26 eekossee exee [εἴκοσι ἕξι]
27 eekossee epta [εἴκοσι ἑπτά]
28 eekossee okto [εἴκοσι ὀκτώ]
29 eekossee enea [εἴκοσι ἐννέα]
30 treeanda [τριάντα]
31 treeanda ena [τριάντα ἕνα]
40 saranda [σαράντα]
50 peneenda [πενήντα]
60 exeenda [ἑξήντα]

70 evthomeenda [ἐβδομήντα]
80 ogthonda [ὀγδόντα]
90 eneneenda [ἐνενήντα]
100 ekato [ἑκατό]
101 ekaton ena [ἑκατόν ἕνα]
165 ekaton exeenda pende
     [ἑκατόν ἑξήντα πέντε]
200 theeakossea [διακόσια]
300 treeakosseea [τριακόσια]
1,000 kheeleea [χίλια]
2,000 theeo kheeleeathes [δύο χιλιάδες]
3,000 trees kheeleeathes [τρεῖς χιλιάδες]
4,655 tesserees kheeleeathes exakosseea
       peneenda pende

NB: *in Greek the comma is a decimal point; for
thousands use a full-stop, eg 6.000*

Dates: *to say the date in Greek just use the ·
ordinary number, eg:*

on the second of ... stees theeo ...

Exceptions are:

on the 1st of ... stees meea
on the 3rd of ... stees trees
on the 4th of ... stees tesserees
on the 13th of ... stees thekatrees
on the 14th of ... stees thekatesserees
on the 21st of ... stees eekossee meea
on the 23rd of ... stees eekossee trees
on the 24th of ... stees eekossee tesserees
on the 31st of ... stees treeanda meea

THE GREEK ALPHABET

Α	α	ἄλφα	ALFA	a *as in Anne*
Β	β	βῆτα	VITA	v
Γ	γ	γάμμα	GAMA	y *as in yes*
Δ	δ	δέλτα	THELTA	th *as in that*
Ε	ε	ἔψιλον	EPSILON	e *as in end*
Ζ	ζ	ζῆτα	ZITA	z *as in zero*
Η	η	ἦτα	ITA	ee
Θ	θ	θῆτα	THITA	th *as in theatre*
Ι	ι	γιῶτα	YOTA	ee
Κ	κ	κάπα	KAPA	k
Λ	λ	λάμδα	LAMTHA	l
Μ	μ	μί	MI	m
Ν	ν	νί	NI	n
Ξ	ξ	ξί	KSI	x
Ο	ο	ὄμικρον	OMIKRON	o
Π	π	πί	PE	p
Ρ	ρ	ρό	RO	r
Σ	σ, ς*	σίγμα	SIGMA	s
Τ	τ	ταῦ	TAF	t
Υ	υ	ὕψιλον	IPSILON	ee
Φ	φ	φί	FI	f
Χ	χ	χί	KHI	ch *as in Scottish loch*
Ψ	ψ	ψί	PSI	ps
Ω	ω	ὠμέγα	OMEGA	o

*used only at the end of a word